Tree and Leaf, whic[h] brings together an [essay] 'story', *Leaf by Nigg[le]* fairy stories have their own literary value and should not be seen either as academic exercises or as stories written specifically for children. His own early short story is an apt and beautiful illustration. The world of Faery is the setting for *Smith of Wootton Major*, which forms the second part of this collection. The preparation of the Great Cake to mark the Feast of Good Children was a human, cheerful occasion, but other less material powers were at work and the world of man and of faery met and blended in a strange, haunting union. Professor Tolkien's dramatic poem *The Homecoming of Beorhtnoth Beorhthelm's Son* concludes the book. It tells, in alliterative, colloquial verse, of the events which followed the rout of the English by Viking invaders in 991. Amid the hopeless prospect of 'ever work and war till the world passes' a sense of hope and spirituality remains.

WITHDRAWN

Also by J. R. R. Tolkien

The Hobbit
The Lord of the Rings
   The Fellowship of the Ring
   The Two Towers
   The Return of the King
The Silmarillion
The Father Christmas Letters
Farmer Giles of Ham
The Adventures of Tom Bombadil
Sir Gawain and the Green Knight, Pearl
   and Sir Orfeo

With Donald Swann
The Road Goes Ever On

Tree and Leaf

Smith of Wootton Major

The Homecoming of Beorhtnoth Beorhthelm's Son

J. R. R. TOLKIEN

I. C. C. LIBRARY

London
UNWIN PAPERBACKS
Boston   Sydney

Tree and Leaf first published in Great Britain by George Allen & Unwin 1964
Reprinted eight times

Smith of Wootton Major first published in Great Britain by George Allen & Unwin 1967
Reprinted six times

The Homecoming of Beorhtnoth Beorhthelm's Son first published in Great Britain by George Allen & Unwin 1975

First published in Unwin Paperbacks 1975
Reprinted 1977, 1979

This book is copyright under the Berne Convention. All rights are reserved. Apart from any fair dealing for the purpose of private study, research, criticism or review, as permitted under the Copyright Act, 1956, no part of this publication may be reproduced, stored in a retrieval system, or transmitted, in any form or by any means, electronic, electrical, chemical, mechanical, optical, photocopying, recording or otherwise, without the prior permission of the copyright owner. Enquiries should be sent to the publishers at the undermentioned address:

UNWIN® PAPERBACKS
40 Museum Street, London WC1A 1LU

© George Allen & Unwin (Publishers) Ltd, 1964, 1967, 1975

British Library Cataloguing in Publication Data

Tolkien, John Ronald Reuel
    Tree and leaf; [and] Smith of Wootton Major; [and],
    The homecoming of Beorhtnoth Beorhthelm's Son.
    1. Title   2. Tolkien, John Ronald Reuel. Smith
    of Wootton Major.   3. Tolkien. John Ronald Reuel.
    The homecoming of Beorhtnoth Beorhthelm's Son
    828'.9'1209   PR6039.032A6   78–40934

    ISBN 0-04-820016-6

Printed in Great Britain by
Cox and Wyman Ltd, London, Reading and Fakenham

Contents

Tree and Leaf

Introductory Note

THESE two things, *On Fairy-Stories* and *Leaf by Niggle*, are here reprinted and issued together. They are no longer easy to obtain, but they may still be found interesting, especially by those to whom *The Lord of the Rings* has given pleasure. Though one is an 'essay' and the other a 'story', they are related: by the symbols of Tree and Leaf, and by both touching in different ways on what is called in the essay 'sub-creation'. Also they were written in the same period (1938–9), when *The Lord of the Rings* was beginning to unroll itself and to unfold prospects of labour and exploration in yet unknown country as daunting to me as to the hobbits. At about that time we had reached Bree, and I had then no more notion than they had of what had become of Gandalf or who Strider was; and I had begun to despair of surviving to find out.

The essay was originally composed as an Andrew Lang Lecture and was in a shorter form delivered in the University of St Andrews in 1938.[1] It was eventually published, with a little enlargement, as one of the items in *Essays presented to Charles Williams*, Oxford University Press, 1947, now out of print. It is here reproduced with only a few minor alterations.

The story was not published until 1947 (*Dublin Review*). It has not been changed since it reached manuscript form,

[1] Not 1940 as incorrectly stated in 1947.

very swiftly, one day when I awoke with it already in mind. One of its sources was a great-limbed poplar tree that I could see even lying in bed. It was suddenly lopped and mutilated by its owner, I do not know why. It is cut down now, a less barbarous punishment for any crimes it may have been accused of, such as being large and alive. I do not think it had any friends, or any mourners, except myself and a pair of owls.

J. R. R. TOLKIEN

On Fairy-Stories

I PROPOSE to speak about fairy-stories, though I am aware that this is a rash adventure. Faërie is a perilous land, and in it are pitfalls for the unwary and dungeons for the overbold. And overbold I may be accounted, for though I have been a lover of fairy-stories since I learned to read, and have at times thought about them, I have not studied them professionally. I have been hardly more than a wandering explorer (or trespasser) in the land, full of wonder but not of information.

The realm of fairy-story is wide and deep and high and filled with many things: all manner of beasts and birds are found there; shoreless seas and stars uncounted; beauty that is an enchantment, and an ever-present peril; both joy and sorrow as sharp as swords. In that realm a man may, perhaps, count himself fortunate to have wandered, but its very richness and strangeness tie the tongue of a traveller who would report them. And while he is there it is dangerous for him to ask too many questions, lest the gates should be shut and the keys be lost.

There are, however, some questions that one who is to speak about fairy-stories must expect to answer, or attempt to answer, whatever the folk of Faërie may think of his impertinence. For instance: What are fairy-stories? What is their origin? What is the use of them?

I will try to give answers to these questions, or such hints of answers to them as I have gleaned – primarily from the stories themselves, the few of all their multitude that I know.

FAIRY-STORY

What is a fairy-story? In this case you will turn to the *Oxford English Dictionary* in vain. It contains no reference to the combination *fairy-story*, and is unhelpful on the subject of *fairies* generally. In the Supplement, *fairy-tale* is recorded since the year 1750, and its leading sense is said to be (*a*) a tale about fairies, or generally a fairy legend; with developed senses, (*b*) an unreal or incredible story, and (*c*) a falsehood.

The last two senses would obviously make my topic hopelessly vast. But the first sense is too narrow. Not too narrow for an essay; it is wide enough for many books, but too narrow to cover actual usage. Especially so, if we accept the lexicographer's definition of *fairies*: 'supernatural beings of diminutive size, in popular belief supposed to possess magical powers and to have great influence for good or evil over the affairs of man'.

Supernatural is a dangerous and difficult word in any of its senses, looser or stricter. But to fairies it can hardly be applied, unless *super* is taken merely as a superlative prefix. For it is man who is, in contrast to fairies, supernatural (and often of diminutive stature); whereas they are natural, far more natural than he. Such is their doom. The road to fairyland is not the road to Heaven; nor even to Hell, I believe, though some have held that it may lead thither indirectly by the Devil's tithe.

O see ye not yon narrow road
    So thick beset wi' thorns and briers?
That is the path of Righteousness,
    Though after it but few inquires.

And see ye not yon braid, braid road
    That lies across the lily leven?
That is the path of Wickedness,
    Though some call it the Road to Heaven.

And see ye not yon bonny road
    That winds about yon fernie brae?
That is the road to fair Elfland,
    Where thou and I this night maun gae.

As for *diminutive size*: I do not deny that the notion is a leading one in modern use. I have often thought that it would be interesting to try to find out how that has come to be so; but my knowledge is not sufficient for a certain answer. Of old there were indeed some inhabitants of Faërie that were small (though hardly diminutive), but smallness was not characteristic of that people as a whole. The diminutive being, elf or fairy, is (I guess) in England largely a sophisticated product of literary fancy.[1] It is perhaps not unnatural that in England, the land where the love of the delicate and fine has often reappeared in art, fancy should in this matter turn towards the dainty and diminutive, as in France it went to court and put on powder and diamonds. Yet I suspect

[1] I am speaking of developments before the growth of interest in the folk-lore of other countries. The English words, such as *elf*, have long been influenced by French (from which *fay* and *faërie*, *fairy* are derived); but in later times, through their use in translation, both *fairy* and *elf* have acquired much of the atmosphere of German, Scandinavian, and Celtic tales, and many characteristics of the *huldu-fólk*, the *daoine-sithe*, and the *tylwyth teg*.

that this flower-and-butterfly minuteness was also a product of 'rationalisation', which transformed the glamour of Elf-land into mere finesse, and invisibility into a fragility that could hide in a cowslip or shrink behind a blade of grass. It seems to become fashionable soon after the great voyages had begun to make the world seem too narrow to hold both men and elves; when the magic land of Hy Breasail in the West had become the mere Brazils, the land of red-dye-wood.[1] In any case it was largely a literary business in which William Shakespeare and Michael Drayton played a part.[2] Drayton's *Nymphidia* is one ancestor of that long line of flower-fairies and fluttering sprites with antennae that I so disliked as a child, and which my children in their turn detested. Andrew Lang had similar feelings. In the preface to the *Lilac Fairy Book* he refers to the tales of tiresome contemporary authors: 'they always begin with a little boy or girl who goes out and meets the fairies of polyanthuses and gardenias and apple-blossom . . . These fairies try to be funny and fail; or they try to preach and succeed.'

But the business began, as I have said, long before the nineteenth century, and long ago achieved tiresomeness, certainly the tiresomeness of trying to be funny and failing. Drayton's *Nymphidia* is, considered as a fairy-story (a story about fairies), one of the worst ever written. The palace of Oberon has walls of spider's legs,

> And windows of the eyes of cats,
> And for the roof, instead of slats,
> Is covered with the wings of bats.

[1] For the probability that the Irish *Hy Breasail* played a part in the naming of Brazil see Nansen, *In Northern Mists*, ii, 223–30.

[2] Their influence was not confined to England. German *Elf, Elfe* appears to be derived from *A Midsummer-night's Dream*, in Wieland's translation (1764).

The knight Pigwiggen rides on a frisky earwig, and sends his love, Queen Mab, a bracelet of emmets' eyes, making an assignation in a cowslip-flower. But the tale that is told amid all this prettiness is a dull story of intrigue and sly go-betweens; the gallant knight and angry husband fall into the mire, and their wrath is stilled by a draught of the waters of Lethe. It would have been better if Lethe had swallowed the whole affair. Oberon, Mab, and Pigwiggen may be diminutive elves or fairies, as Arthur, Guinevere, and Lancelot are not; but the good and evil story of Arthur's court is a 'fairy-story' rather than this tale of Oberon.

Fairy, as a noun more or less equivalent to *elf*, is a relatively modern word, hardly used until the Tudor period. The first quotation in the *Oxford Dictionary* (the only one before A.D. 1450) is significant. It is taken from the poet Gower: *as he were a faierie*. But this Gower did not say. He wrote *as he were of faierie*, 'as if he were come from Faërie'. Gower was describing a young gallant who seeks to bewitch the hearts of the maidens in church.

> His croket kembd and thereon set
> A Nouche with a chapelet,
> Or elles one of grene leves
> Which late com out of the greves,
> Al for he sholde seme freissh;
>
> And thus he loketh on the fleissh,
> Riht as an hauk which hath a sihte
> Upon the foul ther he schal lihte,
> And as he were of faierie
> He scheweth him tofore here yhe.[1]

This is a young man of mortal blood and bone; but he gives

[1] *Confessio Amantis*, v. 7065 ff.

a much better picture of the inhabitants of Elfland than the definition of a 'fairy' under which he is, by a double error, placed. For the trouble with the real folk of Faërie is that they do not always look like what they are; and they put on the pride and beauty that we would fain wear ourselves. At least part of the magic that they wield for the good or evil of man is power to play on the desires of his body and his heart. The Queen of Elfland, who carried off Thomas the Rhymer upon her milk-white steed swifter than the wind, came riding by the Eildon Tree as a lady, if one of enchanting beauty. So that Spenser was in the true tradition when he called the knights of his Faërie by the name of Elfe. It belonged to such knights as Sir Guyon rather than to Pigwiggen armed with a hornet's sting.

Now, though I have only touched (wholly inadequately) on *elves* and *fairies*, I must turn back; for I have digressed from my proper theme: fairy-stories, I said the sense 'stories about fairies' was too narrow.[1] It is too narrow, even if we reject the diminutive size, for fairy-stories are not in normal English usage stories *about* fairies or elves, but stories about Fairy, that is *Faërie*, the realm or state in which fairies have their being. *Faërie* contains many things besides elves and fays, and besides dwarfs, witches, trolls, giants, or dragons: it holds the seas, the sun, the moon, the sky; and the earth, and all things that are in it: tree and bird, water and stone, wine and bread, and ourselves, mortal men, when we are enchanted.

[1] Except in special cases such as collections of Welsh or Gaelic tales. In these the stories about the 'Fair Family' or the Shee-folk are sometimes distinguished as 'fairy-tales' from 'folk-tales' concerning other marvels. In this use 'fairy-tales' or 'fairy-lore' are usually short accounts of the appearances of 'fairies' or their intrusions upon the affairs of men. But this distinction is a product of translation.

Stories that are actually concerned primarily with 'fairies', that is with creatures that might also in modern English be called 'elves', are relatively rare, and as a rule not very interesting. Most good 'fairy-stories' are about the *aventures* of men in the Perilous Realm or upon its shadowy marches. Naturally so; for if elves are true, and really exist independently of our tales about them, then this also is certainly true: elves are not primarily concerned with us, nor we with them. Our fates are sundered, and our paths seldom meet. Even upon the borders of Faërie we encounter them only at some chance crossing of the ways.[1]

The definition of a fairy-story – what it is, or what it should be – does not, then, depend on any definition or historical account of elf or fairy, but upon the nature of *Faërie*: the Perilous Realm itself, and the air that blows in that country. I will not attempt to define that, nor to describe it directly. It cannot be done. Faërie cannot be caught in a net of words; for it is one of its qualities to be indescribable, though not imperceptible. It has many ingredients, but analysis will not necessarily discover the secret of the whole. Yet I hope that what I have later to say about the other questions will give some glimpses of my own imperfect vision of it. For the moment I will say only this: a 'fairy-story' is one which touches on or uses Faërie, whatever its own main purpose may be: satire, adventure, morality, fantasy. Faërie itself may perhaps most nearly be translated by Magic[2] – but it is magic of a peculiar mood and power, at the furthest pole from the vulgar devices of the laborious, scientific, magician. There is one proviso: if there is any

[1] This is true also, even if they are only creations of Man's mind, 'true' only as reflecting in a particular way one of Man's visions of Truth.

[2] See further below, p. 54.

satire present in the tale, one thing must not be made fun of, the magic itself. That must in that story be taken seriously, neither laughed at nor explained away. Of this seriousness the medieval *Sir Gawain and the Green Knight* is an admirable example.

But even if we apply only these vague and ill-defined limits, it becomes plain that many, even the learned in such matters, have used the term 'fairy-tale' very carelessly. A glance at those books of recent times that claim to be collections of 'fairy-stories' is enough to show that tales about fairies, about the fair family in any of its houses, or even about dwarfs and goblins, are only a small part of their content. That, as we have seen, was to be expected. But these books also contain many tales that do not use, do not even touch upon, Faërie at all; that have in fact no business to be included.

I will give one or two examples of the expurgations I would perform. This will assist the negative side of definition. It will also be found to lead on to the second question: what are the origins of fairy-stories?

The number of collections of fairy-stories is now very great. In English none probably rival either the popularity, or the inclusiveness, or the general merits of the twelve books of twelve colours which we owe to Andrew Lang and to his wife. The first of these appeared more than fifty years ago (1889), and is still in print. Most of its contents pass the test more or less clearly. I will not analyse them, though an analysis might be interesting, but I note in passing that of the stories in this *Blue Fairy Book* none are primarily about 'fairies', few refer to them. Most of the tales are taken from French sources: a just choice in some ways at that time, as perhaps it would be still (though not to my taste, now or in childhood). At any rate, so powerful has been the influence of Charles Perrault, since his *Contes de ma Mère l'Oye* were first Englished in the eighteenth century, and of such other excerpts from the vast storehouse of the *Cabinet des Fées* as have become well known, that still, I suppose, if you asked a man to name at random a typical 'fairy-story', he would be most likely to name one of these French things: such as *Puss-in-Boots*, *Cinderella*, or *Little Red Riding Hood*. With some people *Grimm's Fairy Tales* might come first to mind.

But what is to be said of the appearance in the *Blue Fairy Book* of *A Voyage to Lilliput*? I will say this: it is *not* a fairy-story, neither as its author made it, nor as it here appears 'condensed' by Miss May Kendall. It has no business in this place. I fear that it was included merely because Lilliputians are small, even diminutive – the only way in which they are at all remarkable. But smallness is in Faërie, as in our world, only an accident. Pygmies are no nearer to fairies than are Patagonians. I do not rule this story out because of its satirical intent: there is satire, sustained or intermittent, in undoubted fairy-stories, and satire may often have been intended in traditional tales where we do not now perceive it. I rule it out, because the vehicle of the satire, brilliant invention though it may be, belongs to the class of travellers' tales. Such tales report many marvels, but they are marvels to be seen in this mortal world in some region of our own time and space; distance alone conceals them. The tales of Gulliver have no more right of entry than the yarns of Baron Munchausen; or than, say, *The First Men in the Moon* or *The Time-Machine*. Indeed, for the Eloi and the Morlocks there would be a better claim than for the Lilliputians. Lilliputians are merely men peered down at, sardonically, from just above the house-tops. Eloi and Morlocks live far away in an abyss of time so deep as to work an enchantment upon them; and if they are descended from ourselves, it may be remembered that an ancient English thinker once derived the *ylfe*, the very elves, through Cain from Adam.[1] This enchantment of distance, especially of distant time, is weakened only by the preposterous and incredible Time Machine itself. But we see in this example one of the main reasons why the borders of fairy-story are inevitably dubious. The magic of Faërie is not an end in itself, its virtue is in its operations: among these are the satisfaction of certain primordial human desires. One of these desires is to survey the depths of space and time. Another is (as will be seen) to hold communion with other living things. A story may thus deal with the satisfaction of these desires, with or without the operation of either machine or magic, and in proportion as it succeeds it will approach the quality and have the flavour of fairy-story.

Next, after travellers' tales, I would also exclude, or rule out of order, any story that uses the machinery of Dream, the dreaming of actual human sleep, to explain the apparent occurrence of its marvels. At the least, even if the reported dream was in other respects in itself a fairy-story, I would condemn the whole as gravely defective: like a good picture in a disfiguring frame. It is true that Dream is not unconnected with Faërie. In dreams strange powers of the mind may be unlocked. In some of them a man may for a space wield the power of Faërie, that power which, even as it conceives the story, causes it to take living form and colour before the eyes. A real dream may indeed sometimes be a fairy-story of almost elvish ease and skill – while it is being dreamed. But if a waking writer tells you that his tale is only a thing imagined in his sleep, he cheats deliberately the primal desire at the heart of Faërie: the realisation, independent of the conceiving mind, of imagined wonder. It is often reported of fairies (truly or lyingly, I do not know)

[1] *Beowulf*, 111–12.

that they are workers of illusion, that they are cheaters of men by 'fantasy'; but that is quite another matter. That is their affair. Such trickeries happen, at any rate, inside tales in which the fairies are not themselves illusions; behind the fantasy real wills and powers exist, independent of the minds and purposes of men.

It is at any rate essential to a genuine fairy-story, as distinct from the employment of this form for lesser or debased purposes, that it should be presented as 'true'. The meaning of 'true' in this connection I will consider in a moment. But since the fairy-story deals with 'marvels', it cannot tolerate any frame or machinery suggesting that the whole story in which they occur is a figment or illusion. The tale itself may, of course, be so good that one can ignore the frame. Or it may be successful and amusing as a dream-story. So are Lewis Carroll's *Alice* stories, with their dream-frame and dream-transitions. For this (and other reasons) they are not fairy-stories.[1]

There is another type of marvellous tale that I would exclude from the title 'fairy-story', again certainly not because I do not like it: namely pure 'Beast-fable'. I will choose an example from Lang's Fairy Books: *The Monkey's Heart*, a Swahili tale which is given in the *Lilac Fairy Book*. In this story a wicked shark tricked a monkey into riding on his back, and carried him half-way to his own land, before he revealed the fact that the sultan of that country was sick and needed a monkey's heart to cure his disease. But the monkey outwitted the shark, and induced him to return by convincing him that the heart had been left behind at home, hanging in a bag on a tree.

The beast-fable has, of course, a connection with fairy-stories. Beasts and birds and other creatures often talk like

[1] See Note A at the end (p. 72).

men in real fairy-stories. In some part (often small) this marvel derives from one of the primal 'desires' that lie near the heart of Faërie: the desire of men to hold communion with other living things. But the speech of beasts in the beast-fable has developed into a separate branch, has little reference to that desire, and often wholly forgets it. The magical understanding by men of the proper languages of birds and beasts and trees, that is much nearer to the true purposes of Faërie. But in stories in which no human being is concerned; or in which the animals are the heroes and heroines, and men and women, if they appear, are mere adjuncts; and above all those in which the animal form is only a mask upon a human face, a device of the satirist or the preacher, in these we have beast-fable and not fairy-story: whether it be *Reynard the Fox*, or *The Nun's Priest's Tale*, or *Brer Rabbit*, or merely *The Three Little Pigs*. The stories of Beatrix Potter lie near the borders of Faërie, but outside it, I think, for the most part.[1] Their nearness is due largely to their strong moral element: by which I mean their inherent morality, not any allegorical *significatio*. But *Peter Rabbit*, though it contains a prohibition, and though there are prohibitions in fairyland (as, probably, there are throughout the universe on every plane and in every dimension), remains a beast-fable.

Now *The Monkey's Heart* is also plainly only a beast-fable. I suspect that its inclusion in a 'Fairy Book' is due not primarily to its entertaining quality, but precisely to the monkey's heart supposed to have been left behind in a bag. That was significant to Lang, the student of folk-lore, even though this curious idea is here used only as a joke; for, in this

---

[1] *The Tailor of Gloucester* perhaps comes nearest. *Mrs Tiggy-winkle* would be as near, but for the hinted dream-explanation. I would also include *The Wind in the Willows* in beast-fable.

tale, the monkey's heart was in fact quite normal and in his breast. None the less this detail is plainly only a secondary use of an ancient and very widespread folk-lore notion, which does occur in fairy-stories;[1] the notion that the life or strength of a man or creature may reside in some other place or thing; or in some part of the body (especially the heart) that can be detached and hidden in a bag, or under a stone, or in an egg. At one end of recorded folk-lore history this idea was used by George MacDonald in his fairy story *The Giant's Heart*, which derives this central motive (as well as many other details) from well-known traditional tales. At the other end, indeed in what is probably one of the oldest stories in writing, it occurs in *The Tale of the Two Brothers* on the Egyptian D'Orsigny papyrus. There the younger brother says to the elder:

'I shall enchant my heart, and I shall place it upon the top of the flower of the cedar. Now the cedar will be cut down and my heart will fall to the ground, and thou shalt come to seek for it, even though thou pass seven years in seeking it; but when thou has found it, put it into a vase of cold water, and in very truth I shall live.'[2]

But that point of interest and such comparisons as these bring us to the brink of the second question: What are the origins of 'fairy-stories'? That must, of course, mean: the origin or origins of the fairy elements. To ask what is the origin of stories (however qualified) is to ask what is the origin of language and of the mind.

[1] Such as, for instance: *The Giant that had no Heart* in Dasent's *Popular Tales from the Norse*; or *The Sea-Maiden* in Campbell's *Popular Tales of the West Highlands* (no. iv, cf. also no. i); or more remotely *Die Kristallkugel* in Grimm.

[2] Budge, *Egyptian Reading Book*, p. xxi.

ORIGINS

Actually the question: What is the origin of the fairy element? lands us ultimately in the same fundamental inquiry; but there are many elements in fairy-stories (such as this detachable heart, or swan-robes, magic rings, arbitrary prohibitions, wicked step-mothers, and even fairies themselves) that can be studied without tackling this main question. Such studies are, however, scientific (at least in intent); they are the pursuit of folklorists or anthropologists: that is of people using the stories not as they were meant to be used, but as a quarry from which to dig evidence, or information, about matters in which they are interested. A perfectly legitimate procedure in itself – but ignorance or forgetfulness of the nature of a story (as a thing told in its entirety) has often led such inquirers into strange judgements. To investigators of this sort recurring similarities (such as this matter of the heart) seem specially important. So much so that students of folk-lore are apt to get off their own proper track, or to express themselves in a misleading 'shorthand': misleading in particular, if it gets out of their monographs into books about literature. They are inclined to say that any two stories that are built round the same folk-lore motive, or are made up of a generally similar combination of such motives, are 'the same stories'. We read that *Beowulf* 'is only a version of *Dat Erdmänneken*'; that '*The Black Bull of Norroway* is *Beauty and the Beast*', or 'is the same story as *Eros and Psyche*'; that the Norse *Mastermaid* (or the Gaelic *Battle of the Birds*[1] and its many congeners and variants) is 'the same story as the Greek tale of Jason and Medea'.

[1] See Campbell, op. cit., vol. i.

Statements of that kind may express (in undue abbreviation) some element of truth; but they are not true in a fairy-story sense, they are not true in art or literature. It is precisely the colouring, the atmosphere, the unclassifiable individual details of a story, and above all the general purport that informs with life the undissected bones of the plot, that really count. Shakespeare's *King Lear* is not the same as Layamon's story in his *Brut*. Or to take the extreme case of *Red Riding Hood*: it is of merely secondary interest that the re-told versions of this story, in which the little girl is saved by wood-cutters, is directly derived from Perrault's story in which she was eaten by the wolf. The really important thing is that the later version has a happy ending (more or less, and if we do not mourn the grandmother overmuch), and that Perrault's version had not. And that is a very profound difference, to which I shall return.

Of course, I do not deny, for I feel strongly, the fascination of the desire to unravel the intricately knotted and ramified history of the branches on the Tree of Tales. It is closely connected with the philologists' study of the tangled skein of Language, of which I know some small pieces. But even with regard to language it seems to me that the essential quality and aptitudes of a given language in a living monument is both more important to seize and far more difficult to make explicit than its linear history. So with regard to fairy stories, I feel that it is more interesting, and also in its way more difficult, to consider what they are, what they have become for us, and what values the long alchemic processes of time have produced in them. In Dasent's words I would say: 'We must be satisfied with the soup that is set before us, and not desire to see the bones of the ox out of which it has been boiled.'[1] Though, oddly enough, Dasent by 'the soup' meant

[1] *Popular Tales from the Norse*, p. xviii.

a mishmash of bogus pre-history founded on the early surmises of Comparative Philology; and by 'desire to see the bones' he meant a demand to see the workings and the proofs that led to these thoeries. By 'the soup' I mean the story as it is served up by its author or teller, and by 'the bones' its sources or material – even when (by rare luck) those can be with certainty discovered. But I do not, of course, forbid criticism of the soup as soup.

I shall therefore pass lightly over the question of origins. I am too unlearned to deal with it in any other way; but it is the least important of the three questions for my purpose, and a few remarks will suffice. It is plain enough that fairy-stories (in wider or in narrower sense) are very ancient indeed. Related things appear in very early records; and they are found universally, wherever there is language. We are therefore obviously confronted with a variant of the problem that the archaeologist encounters, or the comparative philologist: with the debate between *independent evolution* (or rather *invention*) of the similar; *inheritance* from a common ancestry; and *diffusion* at various times from one or more centres. Most debates depend on an attempt (by one or both sides) at over-simplification; and I do not suppose that this debate is an exception. The history of fairy-stories is probably more complex than the physical history of the human race, and as complex as the history of human language. All three things: independent invention, inheritance, and diffusion, have evidently played their part in producing the intricate web of Story. It is now beyond all skill but that of the elves to unravel it.[1] Of these three *invention* is the most important

---

[1] Except in particularly fortunate cases; or in a few occasional details. It is indeed easier to unravel a single *thread* – an incident, a name, a motive – than to trace the history of any *picture* defined by many threads. For with the picture in the tapestry a new element

and fundamental, and so (not surprisingly) also the most mysterious. To an inventor, that is to a storymaker, the other two must in the end lead back. *Diffusion* (borrowing in space), whether of an artefact or a story, only refers the problem of origin elsewhere. At the centre of the supposed diffusion there is a place where once an inventor lived. Similarly with *inheritance* (borrowing in time): in this way we arrive at last only at an ancestral inventor. While if we believe that sometimes there occurred the independent striking out of similar ideas and themes or devices, we simply multiply the ancestral inventor but do not in that way the more clearly understand his gift.

Philology has been dethroned from the high place it once had in this court of inquiry. Max Müller's view of mythology as a 'disease of language' can be abandoned without regret. Mythology is not a disease at all, though it may like all human things become diseased. You might as well say that thinking is a disease of the mind. It would be more near the truth to say that languages, especially modern European languages, are a disease of mythology. But Language cannot, all the same, be dismissed. The incarnate mind, the tongue, and the tale are in our world coeval. The human mind, endowed with the powers of generalisation and abstraction, sees not only *green-grass*, discriminating it from other things (and finding it fair to look upon), but sees that it is *green* as well as being *grass*. But how powerful, how stimulating to the very faculty that produced it, was the invention of the adjective: no spell or incantation in Faërie is more potent.

---

has come in: the picture is greater than, and not explained by, the the sum of the component threads. Therein lies the inherent weakness of the analytic (or 'scientific') method: it finds out much about things that occur in stories, but little or nothing about their effect in any given story.

And that is not surprising: such incantations might indeed be said to be only another view of adjectives, a part of speech in a mythical grammar. The mind that thought of *light, heavy, grey, yellow, still, swift*, also conceived of magic that would make heavy things light and able to fly, turn grey lead into yellow gold, and the still rock into swift water. If it could do the one, it could do the other; it inevitably did both. When we can take green from grass, blue from heaven, and red from blood, we have already an enchanter's power – upon one plane; and the desire to wield that power in the world external to our minds awakes. It does not follow that we shall use that power well upon any plane. We may put a deadly green upon a man's face and produce a horror; we may make the rare and terrible blue moon to shine; or we may cause woods to spring with silver leaves and rams to wear fleeces of gold, and put hot fire into the belly of the cold worm. But in such 'fantasy', as it is called, new form is made; Faërie begins; Man becomes a sub-creator.

An essential power of Faërie is thus the power of making immediately effective by the will the visions of 'fantasy'. Not all are beautiful or even wholesome, not at any rate the fantasies of fallen Man. And he has stained the elves who have this power (in verity or fable) with his own stain. This aspect of 'mythology' – sub-creation, rather than either representation or symbolic interpretation of the beauties and terrors of the world – is, I think, too little considered. Is that because it is seen rather in Faërie than upon Olympus? Because it is thought to belong to the 'lower mythology' rather than to the 'higher'? There has been much debate concerning the relations of these things, of *folk-tale* and *myth*; but, even if there had been no debate, the question would require some notice in any consideration of origins, however brief.

At one time it was a dominant view that all such matter was derived from 'nature-myths'. The Olympians were *personifications* of the sun, of dawn, of night, and so on, and all the stories told about them were originally *myths* (*allegories* would have been a better word) of the greater elemental changes and processes of nature. Epic, heroic legend, saga, then localised these stories in real places and humanised them by attributing them to ancestral heroes, mightier than men and yet already men. And finally these legends, dwindling down, became folk-tales, *Märchen*, fairy-stories – nursery-tales.

That would seem to be the truth almost upside down. The nearer the so-called 'nature-myth', or allegory of the large processes of nature, is to its supposed archetype, the less interesting it is, and indeed the less is it of a myth capable of throwing any illumination whatever on the world. Let us assume for the moment, as this theory assumes, that nothing actually exists corresponding to the 'gods' of mythology: no personalities, only astronomical or meteorological objects. Then these natural objects can only be arrayed with a personal significance and glory by a gift, the gift of a person, of a man. Personality can only be derived from a person. The gods may derive their colour and beauty from the high splendours of nature, but it was Man who obtained these for them, abstracted them from sun and moon and cloud; their personality they get direct from him; the shadow or flicker of divinity that is upon them they receive through him from the invisible world, the Supernatural. There is no fundamental distinction between the higher and lower mythologies. Their peoples live, if they live at all, by the same life, just as in the mortal world do kings and peasants.

Let us take what looks like a clear case of Olympian nature-myth: the Norse god Thórr. His name is Thunder, of which

Thórr is the Norse form; and it is not difficult to interpret his hammer, Miöllnir, as lightning. Yet Thórr has (as far as our late records go) a very marked character, or personality, which cannot be found in thunder or in lightning, even though some details can, as it were, be related to these natural phenomena: for instance, his red beard, his loud voice and violent temper, his blundering and smashing strength. None the less it is asking a question without much meaning, if we inquire: Which came first, nature-allegories about personalised thunder in the mountains, splitting rocks and trees; or stories about an irascible, not very clever, red-beard farmer, of a strength beyond common measure, a person (in all but mere stature) very like the Northern farmers, the *bœndr* by whom Thórr was chiefly beloved? To a picture of such a man Thórr may be held to have 'dwindled', or from it the god may be held to have been enlarged. But I doubt whether either view is right – not by itself, not if you insist that one of these things must precede the other. It is more reasonable to suppose that the farmer popped up in the very moment when Thunder got a voice and face; that there was a distant growl of thunder in the hills every time a story-teller heard a farmer in a rage.

Thórr must, of course, be reckoned a member of the higher aristocracy of mythology: one of the rulers of the world. Yet the tale that is told of him in *Thrymskvitha* (in the Elder Edda) is certainly just a fairy-story. It is old, as far as Norse poems go, but that is not far back (say A.D. 900 or a little earlier, in this case). But there is no real reason for supposing that this tale is 'unprimitive', at any rate in quality: that is, because it is of folk-tale kind and not very dignified. If we could go backwards in time, the fairy-story might be found to change in details, or to give way to other tales. But there would always be a 'fairy-tale' as long as there was any Thórr. When the fairy-tale ceased, there would be just thunder, which no human ear had yet heard.

Something really 'higher' is occasionally glimpsed in mythology: Divinity, the right to power (as distinct from its possession), the due of worship; in fact 'religion'. Andrew Lang said, and is by some still commended for saying,[1] that mythology and religion (in the strict sense of that word) are two distinct things that have become inextricably entangled, though mythology is in itself almost devoid of religious significance.[2]

Yet these things have in fact become entangled – or maybe they were sundered long ago and have since groped slowly, through a labyrinth of error, through confusion, back towards re-fusion. Even fairy-stories as a whole have three faces: the Mystical towards the Supernatural; the Magical towards Nature; and the Mirror of scorn and pity towards Man. The essential face of Faërie is the middle one, the Magical. But the degree in which the others appear (if at all) is variable, and may be decided by the individual story-teller. The Magical, the fairy-story, may be used as a *Mirour de l'Omme*; and it may (but not so easily) be made a vehicle of Mystery. This at least is what George MacDonald attempted, achieving stories of power and beauty when he succeeded, as in *The Golden Key* (which he called a fairy-tale); and even

---

[1] For example, by Christopher Dawson in *Progress and Religion*.

[2] This is borne out by the more careful and sympathetic study of 'primitive' peoples: that is, peoples still living in an inherited paganism, who are not, as we say, civilised. The hasty survey finds only their wilder tales; a closer examination finds their cosmological myths; only patience and inner knowledge discovers their philosophy and religion: the truly worshipful, of which the 'gods' are not necessarily an embodiment at all, or only in a variable measure (often decided by the individual).

when he partly failed, as in *Lilith* (which he called a romance).

For a moment let us return to the 'Soup' that I mentioned above. Speaking of the history of stories and especially of fairy-stories we may say that the Pot of Soup, the Cauldron of Story, has always been boiling, and to it have continually been added new bits, dainty and undainty. For this reason, to take a casual example, the fact that a story resembling the one known as *The Goosegirl* (*Die Gänsemagd* in Grimm) is told in the thirteenth century of Bertha Broadfoot, mother of Charlemagne, really proves nothing either way: neither that the story was (in the thirteenth century) descended from Olympus or Asgard by way of an already legendary king of old, on its way to become a *Hausmärchen*; nor that it was on its way up. The story is found to be widespread, unattached to the mother of Charlemagne or to any historical character. From this fact by itself we certainly cannot deduce that it is not true of Charlemagne's mother, though that is the kind of deduction that is most frequently made from that kind of evidence. The opinion that the story is not true of Bertha Broadfoot must be founded on something else: on features in the story which the critic's philosophy does not allow to be possible in 'real life', so that he would actually disbelieve the tale, even if it were found nowhere else; or on the existence of good historical evidence that Bertha's actual life was quite different, so that he would disbelieve the tale, even if his philosophy allowed that it was perfectly possible in 'real life'. No one, I fancy, would discredit a story that the Archbishop of Canterbury slipped on a banana skin merely because he found that a similar comic mishap had been reported of many people, and especially of elderly gentlemen of dignity. He might disbelieve the story, if he discovered that in it an angel (or even a fairy) had warned the Archbishop that he would slip if he wore gaiters on a Friday. He might also disbelieve the story, if it was stated to have occurred in the period between, say, 1940 and 1945. So much for that. It is an obvious point, and it has been made before; but I venture to make it again (although it is a little beside my present purpose), for it is constantly neglected by those who concern themselves with the origins of tales.

But what of the banana skin? Our business with it really only begins when it has been rejected by historians. It is more useful when it has been thrown away. The historian would be likely to say that the banana-skin story 'became attached to the Archbishop', as he does say on fair evidence that 'the Goosegirl *Märchen* became attached to Berthá'. That way of putting it is harmless enough, in what is commonly known as 'history'. But is it really a good description of what is going on and has gone on in the history of story-making? I do not think so. I think it would be nearer the truth to say that the Archbishop became attached to the banana skin, or that Bertha was turned into the Goosegirl. Better still: I would say that Charlemagne's mother and the Archbishop were put into the Pot, in fact got into the Soup. They were just new bits added to the stock. A considerable honour, for in that soup were many things older, more potent, more beautiful, comic, or terrible than they were in themselves (considered simply as figures of history).

It seems fairly plain that Arthur, once historical (but perhaps as such not of great importance), was also put into the Pot. There he was boiled for a long time, together with many other older figures and devices, of mythology and Faërie, and even some other stray bones of history (such as Alfred's defence against the Danes), until he emerged as a King of Faërie. The situation is similar in the great Northern 'Arthurian' court of the Shield-Kings of Denmark, the *Scyldingas* of ancient English tradition. King Hrothgar and his family have many manifest marks of true history, far more than Arthur; yet even in the older (English) accounts of them they are associated with many figures and events of fairy-story: they have been in the Pot. But I refer now to the remnants of the oldest recorded English tales of Faërie (or its borders), in spite of the fact that they are little known in England, not to discuss the turning of the bear-boy into the knight Beowulf, or to explain the intrusion of the ogre Grendel into the royal hall of Hrothgar. I wish to point to something else that these traditions contain: a singularly suggestive example of the relation of the 'fairy-tale element' to gods and kings and nameless men, illustrating (I believe) the view that this element does not rise or fall, but is there, in the Cauldron of Story, waiting for the great figures of Myth and History, and for the yet nameless He or She, waiting for the moment when they are cast into the simmering stew, one by one or all together, without consideration of rank or precedence.

The great enemy of King Hrothgar was Froda, King of the Heathobards. Yet of Hrothgar's daughter Freawaru we hear echoes of a strange tale – not a usual one in Northern heroic legend: the son of the enemy of her house, Ingeld son of Froda, fell in love with her and wedded her, disastrously. But that is extremely interesting and significant. In the background of the ancient feud looms the figure of that god whom the Norsemen called Frey (the Lord) or Yngvi-frey, and the Angles called Ing: a god of the ancient Northern mythology (and religion) of Fertility and Corn. The enmity of the royal houses was connected with the sacred site of a cult of that religion. Ingeld and his father bear names belonging to it. Freawaru herself is named 'Protection of the Lord (of Frey)'. Yet one of the chief things told later (in Old Icelandic) about Frey is the story in which he falls in love from afar with the daughter of the enemies of the gods, Gerdr, daughter of the giant Gymir, and weds her. Does this prove that Ingeld and Freawaru, or their love, are 'merely mythical'? I think not. History often resembles 'Myth', because they are both ultimately of the same stuff. If indeed Ingeld and Freawaru never lived, or at least never loved, then it is ultimately from nameless man and woman that they get their tale, or rather into whose tale they have entered. They have been put into the Cauldron, where so many potent things lie simmering agelong on the fire, among them Love-at-first-sight. So too of the god. If no young man had ever fallen in love by chance meeting with a maiden, and found old enmities to stand between him and his love, then the god Frey would never have seen Gerdr the giant's daughter from the high-seat of Odin. But if we speak of a Cauldron, we must not wholly forget the Cooks. There are many things in the Cauldron, but the Cooks do not dip in the ladle quite blindly. Their selection is important. The gods are after all gods, and it is a matter of some moment what stories are told of them. So we must freely admit that a tale of love is more likely to be told of a prince in history, indeed is more likely actually to happen in an historical family whose traditions are those of Golden Frey and the Vanir, rather than those of Odin the Goth, the Necromancer, glutter of the crows, Lord of the Slain. Small wonder that *spell* means both a story told, and a formula of power over living men.

But when we have done all that research – collection and comparison of the tales of many lands – can do; when we have explained many of the elements commonly found embedded in fairy-stories (such as stepmothers, enchanted bears and bulls, cannibal witches, taboos on names, and the like) as relics of ancient customs once practised in daily life, or of beliefs once held as beliefs and not as 'fancies' – there remains still a point too often forgotten: that is the effect produced *now* by these old things in the stories as they are.

For one thing they are now *old*, and antiquity has an appeal in itself. The beauty and horror of *The Juniper Tree* (*Von dem Machandelbloom*), with its exquisite and tragic beginning, the abominable cannibal stew, the gruesome bones, the gay and vengeful bird-spirit coming out of a mist that rose from the tree, has remained with me since childhood; and yet always the chief flavour of that tale lingering in the memory was not beauty or horror, but distance and a great abyss of time, not measurable even by *twe tusend Johr*. Without the stew and the bones – which children are now too often spared in mollified versions of Grimm[1] – that vision would largely have been lost. I do not think I was harmed by the horror *in the fairy-tale setting*, out of whatever dark beliefs and practices of the past it may have come. Such stories have now a mythical or total (unanalysable) effect, an effect quite independent of the findings of Comparative Folk-lore, and one which it cannot spoil or explain; they open a door on Other Time, and if we pass through, though only for a moment, we stand outside our own time, outside Time itself, maybe.

If we pause, not merely to note that such old elements have been preserved, but to think *how* they have been preserved, we must conclude, I think, that it has happened, often if not always, precisely because of this literary effect. It cannot have been we, or even the brothers Grimm, that first felt it. Fairy-stories are by no means rocky matrices out of which the fossils cannot be prised except by an expert geologist. The ancient elements can be knocked out, or forgotten and dropped out, or replaced by other ingredients with the greatest

[1] They should not be spared it – unless they are spared the whole story until their digestions are stronger.

ease: as any comparison of a story with closely related variants will show. The things that are there must often have been retained (or inserted) because the oral narrators, instinctively or consciously, felt their literary 'significance'[1]. Even where a prohibition in a fairy-story is guessed to be derived from some taboo once practised long ago, it has probably been preserved in the later stages of the tale's history because of the great mythical significance of prohibition. A sense of that significance may indeed have lain behind some of the taboos themselves. Thou shalt not – or else thou shalt depart beggared into endless regret. The gentlest 'nursery-tales' know it. Even Peter Rabbit was forbidden a garden, lost his blue coat, and took sick. The Locked Door stands as an eternal Temptation.

CHILDREN

I will now turn to children, and so come to the last and most important of the three questions: what, if any, are the values and functions of fairy-stories *now*? It is usually assumed that children are the natural or the specially appropriate audience for fairy-stories. In describing a fairy-story which they think adults might possibly read for their own entertainment, reviewers frequently indulge in such waggeries as: 'this book is for children from the ages of six to sixty'. But I have never yet seen the puff of a new motor-model that began thus: 'this toy will amuse infants from seventeen to seventy'; though that to my mind would be much more appropriate. Is there any *essential* connection between children and fairy-stories? Is there any call for comment, if an adult reads them for himself? *Reads* them as tales, that is, not *studies* them as

[1] See Note B at end (p. 73).

curios. Adults are allowed to collect and study anything, even old theatre-programmes or paper bags.

Among those who still have enough wisdom not to think fairy-stories pernicious, the common opinion seems to be that there is a natural connection between the minds of children and fairy-stories, of the same order as the connection between children's bodies and milk. I think this is an error; at best an error of false sentiment, and one that is therefore most often made by those who, for whatever private reason (such as childlessness), tend to think of children as a special kind of creature, almost a different race, rather than as normal, if immature, members of a particular family, and of the human family at large.

Actually, the association of children and fairy-stories is an accident of our domestic history. Fairy-stories have in the modern lettered world been relegated to the 'nursery', as shabby or old-fashioned furniture is relegated to the play-room, primarily because the adults do not want it, and do not mind if it is misused.[1] It is not the choice of the children which decides this. Children as a class – except in a common lack of experience they are not one – neither like fairy-stories more, nor understand them better than adults do; and no more than they like many other things. They are young and growing, and normally have keen appetites, so the fairy-stories as a rule go down well enough. But in fact only some

[1] In the case of stories and other nursery lore, there is also another factor. Wealthier families employed women to look after their children, and the stories were provided by these nurses, who were sometimes in touch with rustic and traditional lore forgotten by their 'betters'. It is long since this source dried up, at any rate in England; but it once had some importance. But again there is no proof of the special fitness of children as the recipients of this vanishing 'folk-lore'. The nurses might just as well (or better) have been left to choose the pictures and furniture.

children, and some adults, have any special taste for them; and when they have it, it is not exclusive, nor even necessarily dominant.[1] It is a taste, too, that would not appear, I think, very early in childhood without artificial stimulus; it is certainly one that does not decrease but increases with age, if it is innate.

It is true that in recent times fairy-stories have usually been written or 'adapted' for children. But so may music be, or verse, or novels, or history, or scientific manuals. It is a dangerous process, even when it is necessary. It is indeed only saved from disaster by the fact that the arts and sciences are not as a whole relegated to the nursery; the nursery and schoolroom are merely given such tastes and glimpses of the adult thing as seem fit for them in adult opinion (often much mistaken). Any one of these things would, if left altogether in the nursery, become gravely impaired. So would a beautiful table, a good picture, or a useful machine (such as a microscope), be defaced or broken, if it were left long unregarded in a schoolroom. Fairy-stories banished in this way, cut off from a full adult art, would in the end be ruined; indeed in so far as they have been so banished, they have been ruined.

The value of fairy-stories is thus not, in my opinion, to be found by considering children in particular. Collections of fairy-stories are, in fact, by nature attics and lumber-rooms, only by temporary and local custom play-rooms. Their contents are disordered, and often battered, a jumble of different dates, purposes, and tastes; but among them may occasionally be found a thing of permanent virtue: an old work of art, not too much damaged, that only stupidity would ever have stuffed away.

Andrew Lang's *Fairy Books* are not, perhaps, lumber-rooms. They are more like stalls in a rummage-sale. Someone

[1] See Note C at end (p. 74).

with a duster and a fair eye for things that retain some value has been round the attics and box-rooms. His collections are largely a by-product of his adult study of mythology and folk-lore; but they were made into and presented as books for children.[1] Some of the reasons that Lang gave are worth considering.

The introduction to the first of the series speaks of 'children to whom and for whom they are told'. 'They represent', he says, 'the young age of man true to his early loves, and have his unblunted edge of belief, a fresh appetite for marvels.' ' "Is it true?" ' he says, 'is the great question children ask.'

I suspect that *belief* and *appetite for marvels* are here regarded as identical or as closely related. They are radically different, though the appetite for marvels is not at once or at first differentiated by a growing human mind from its general appetite. It seems fairly clear that Lang was using belief in its ordinary sense: belief that a thing exists or can happen in the real (primary) world. If so, then I fear that Lang's words, stripped of sentiment, can only imply that the teller of marvellous tales to children, must or may, or at any rate does trade on their *credulity*, on the lack of experience which makes it less easy for children to distinguish fact from fiction in particular cases, though the distinction in itself is fundamental to the sane human mind, and to fairy-stories.

Children are capable, of course, of *literary belief*, when the story-maker's art is good enough to produce it. That state of mind has been called 'willing suspension of disbelief'. But this does not seem to me a good description of what happens. What really happens is that the story-maker proves a successful 'sub-creator'. He makes a Secondary World which

[1] By Lang and his helpers. It is not true of the majority of the contents in their original (or oldest surviving) forms.

your mind can enter. Inside it, what he relates is 'true': it
accords with the laws of that world. You therefore believe
it, while you are, as it were, inside. The moment disbelief
arises, the spell is broken; the magic, or rather art, has failed.
You are then out in the Primary World again, looking at the
little abortive Secondary World from outside. If you are
obliged, by kindliness or circumstance, to stay, then disbelief
must be suspended (or stifled), otherwise listening and looking would become intolerable. But this suspension of disbelief is a substitute for the genuine thing, a subterfuge we
use when condescending to games or make-believe, or when
trying (more or less willingly) to find what virtue we can in
the work of an art that has for us failed.

A real enthusiast for cricket is in the enchanted state:
Secondary Belief. I, when I watch a match, am on the lower
level. I can achieve (more or less) willing suspension of disbelief, when I am held there and supported by some other
motive that will keep away boredom: for instance, a wild,
heraldic, preference for dark blue rather than light. This
suspension of disbelief may thus be a somewhat tired, shabby,
or sentimental state of mind, and so lean to the 'adult'. I
fancy it is often the state of adults in the presence of a fairy-
story. They are held there and supported by sentiment
(memories of childhood, or notions of what childhood ought
to be like); they think they ought to like the tale. But if they
really liked it, for itself, they would not have to suspend
disbelief: they would believe – in this sense.

Now if Lang had meant anything like this there might have
been some truth in his words. It may be argued that it is
easier to work the spell with children. Perhaps it is, though
I am not sure of this. The appearance that it is so is often, I
think, an adult illusion produced by children's humility,
their lack of critical experience and vocabulary, and their

voracity (proper to their rapid growth). They like or try to like what is given to them: if they do not like it, they cannot well express their dislike or give reasons for it (and so may conceal it); and they like a great mass of different things indiscriminately, without troubling to analyse the planes of their belief. In any case I doubt if this potion – the enchantment of the effective fairy-story – is really one of the kind that becomes 'blunted' by use, less potent after repeated draughts.

' "Is it true?" is the great question children ask', Lang said. They do ask that question, I know; and it is not one to be rashly or idly answered.[1] But that question is hardly evidence of 'unblunted belief', or even of the desire for it. Most often it proceeds from the child's desire to know which kind of literature he is faced with. Children's knowledge of the world is often so small that they cannot judge, off-hand and without help, between the fantastic, the strange (that is rare or remote facts), the nonsensical, and the merely 'grown-up' (that is ordinary things of their parents' world, much of which still remains unexplored). But they recognise the different classes, and may like all of them at times. Of course the borders between them are often fluctuating or confused; but that is not only true for children. We all know the differences in kind, but we are not always sure how to place anything that we hear. A child may well believe a report that there are ogres in the next county; many grown-up persons find it easy to believe of another country; and as for another planet, very few adults seem able to imagine it as peopled, if at all, by anything but monsters of iniquity.

[1] Far more often they have asked me: 'Was he good? Was he wicked?' That is, they were more concerned to get the Right side and the Wrong side clear. For that is a question equally important in History and in Faërie.

Now I was one of the children whom Andrew Lang was addressing – I was born at about the same time as the *Green Fairy Book* – the children for whom he seemed to think that fairy-stories were the equivalent of the adult novel, and of whom he said: 'Their taste remains like the taste of their naked ancestors thousands of years ago; and they seem to like fairy-tales better than history, poetry, geography, or arithmetic.'[1] But do we really know much about these 'naked ancestors', except that they were certainly not naked? Our fairy-stories, however old certain elements in them may be, are certainly not the same as theirs. Yet if it is assumed that we have fairy-stories because they did, then probably we have history, geography, poetry, and arithmetic because they like these things too, as far as they could get them, and in so far as they had yet separated the many branches of their general interest in everything.

And as for children of the present day, Lang's description does not fit my own memories, or my experience of children. Lang may have been mistaken about the children he knew, but if he was not, then at any rate children differ considerably, even within the narrow borders of Britain, and such generalisations which treat them as a class (disregarding their individual talents, and the influences of the countryside they live in, and their upbringing) are delusory. I had no special 'wish to believe'. I wanted to know. Belief depended on the way in which stories were presented to me, by older people, or by the authors, or on the inherent tone and quality of the tale. But at no time can I remember that the enjoyment of a story was dependent on belief that such things could happen, or had happened, in 'real life'. Fairy-stories were plainly not primarily concerned with possibility, but with desirability. If they awakened *desire*, satisfying it while often

[1] Preface to the *Violet Fairy Book*.

whetting it unbearably, they succeeded. It is not necessary to be more explicit here, for I hope to say something later about this desire, a complex of many ingredients, some universal, some particular to modern men (including modern children), or even to certain kinds of men. I had no desire to have either dreams or adventures like *Alice*, and the account of them merely amused me. I had very little desire to look for buried treasure or fight pirates, and *Treasure Island* left me cool. Red Indians were better: there were bows and arrows (I had and have a wholly unsatisfied desire to shoot well with a bow), and strange languages, and glimpses of an archaic mode of life, and, above all, forests in such stories. But the land of Merlin and Arthur was better than these, and best of all the nameless North of Sigurd of the Völsungs, and the prince of all dragons. Such lands were pre-eminently desirable. I never imagined that the dragon was of the same order as the horse. And that was not solely because I saw horses daily, but never even the footprint of a worm.[1] The dragon had the trade-mark *Of Faërie* written plain upon him. In whatever world he had his being it was an Other-world. Fantasy, the making or glimpsing of Other-worlds, was the heart of the desire of Faërie. I desired dragons with a profound desire. Of course, I in my timid body did not wish to have them in the neighbourhood, intruding into my relatively safe world, in which it was, for instance, possible to read stories in peace of mind, free from fear.[2] But the world that contained even the imagination of Fáfnir was richer and more beautiful, at whatever cost of peril.

[1] See Note D at end (p. 75).
[2] This is, naturally, often enough what children mean when they ask: 'Is it true?' They mean: 'I like this, but is it contemporary? Am I safe in my bed?' The answer: 'There is certainly no dragon in England today', is all that they want to hear.

The dweller in the quiet and fertile plains may hear of the tormented hills and the unharvested sea and long for them in his heart. For the heart is hard though the body be soft.

All the same, important as I now perceive the fairy-story element in early reading to have been, speaking for myself as a child, I can only say that a liking for fairy-stories was not a dominant characteristic of early taste. A real taste for them awoke after 'nursery' days, and after the years, few but long-seeming, between learning to read and going to school. In that (I nearly wrote 'happy' or 'golden', it was really a sad and troublous) time I liked many other things as well, or better: such as history, astronomy, botany, grammar, and etymology. I agreed with Lang's generalised 'children' not at all in principle, and only in some points by accident: I was, for instance, insensitive to poetry, and skipped it if it came in tales. Poetry I discovered much later in Latin and Greek, and especially through being made to try and translate English verse into classical verse. A real taste for fairy-stories was wakened by philology on the threshold of manhood, and quickened to full life by war.

I have said, perhaps, more than enough on this point. At least it will be plain that in my opinion fairy-stories should not be *specially* associated with children. They are associated with them: naturally, because children are human and fairy-stories are a natural human taste (though not necessarily a universal one); accidentally, because fairy-stories are a large part of the literary lumber that in latter-day Europe has been stuffed away in attics; unnaturally, because of erroneous sentiment about children, a sentiment that seems to increase with the decline in children.

It is true that the age of childhood-sentiment has produced some delightful books (especially charming, however, to adults) of the fairy kind or near to it; but it has also produced a dreadful undergrowth of stories written or adapted to what was or is conceived to be the measure of children's minds and needs. The old stories are mollified or bowdlerised, instead of being reserved; the imitations are often merely silly, Pigwiggenry without even the intrigue; or patronising; or (deadliest of all) covertly sniggering, with an eye on the other grown-ups present. I will not accuse Andrew Lang of sniggering, but certainly he smiled to himself, and certainly too often he had an eye on the faces of other clever people over the heads of his child-audience – to the very grave detriment of the *Chronicles of Pantouflia*.

Dasent replied with vigour and justice to the prudish critics of his translations from Norse popular tales. Yet he committed the astonishing folly of particularly *forbidding* children to read the last two in his collection. That a man could study fairy-stories and not learn better than that seems almost incredible. But neither criticism, rejoinder, nor prohibition would have been necessary if children had not unnecessarily been regarded as the inevitable readers of the book.

I do not deny that there is a truth in Andrew Lang's words (sentimental though they may sound): 'He who would enter into the Kingdom of Faërie should have the heart of a little child.' For that possession is necessary to all high adventure, into kingdoms both less and far greater than Faërie. But humility and innocence – these things 'the heart of a child' must mean in such a context – do not necessarily imply an uncritical wonder, nor indeed an uncritical tenderness. Chesterton once remarked that the children in whose company he saw Maeterlinck's *Blue Bird* were dissatisfied 'because it did not end with a Day of Judgement, and it was not revealed to the hero and the heroine that the Dog had been faithful and the Cat faithless'. 'For children', he says, 'are innocent and love justice; while most of us are wicked and naturally prefer mercy.'

Andrew Lang was confused on this point. He was at pains to defend the slaying of the Yellow Dwarf by Prince Ricardo in one of his own fairy-stories. 'I hate cruelty,' he said, '. . . but that was in fair fight, sword in hand, and the dwarf, peace to his ashes! died in harness.' Yet it is not clear that 'fair fight' is less cruel than 'fair judgement'; or that piercing a dwarf with a sword is more just than the execution of wicked kings and evil stepmothers – which Lang abjures: he sends the criminals (as he boasts) to retirement on ample pensions. That is mercy untempered by justice. It is true that this plea was not addressed to children but to parents and guardians, to whom Lang was recommending his own *Prince Prigio* and *Prince Ricardo* as suitable for their charges.[1] It is parents and guardians who have classified fairy-stories as *Juvenilia*. And this is a small sample of the falsification of values that results.

If we use *child* in a good sense (it has also legitimately a bad one) we must not allow that to push us into the sentimentality of only using *adult* or *grown-up* in a bad sense (it has also legitimately a good one). The process of growing older is not necessarily allied to growing wickeder, though the two do often happen together. Children are meant to grow up, and not to become Peter Pans. Not to lose innocence and wonder; but to proceed on the appointed journey: that journey upon which it is certainly not better to travel hopefully than to arrive, though we must travel hopefully if we are to arrive. But it is one of the lessons of fairy-stories (if we can speak of the lessons of things that do not lecture) that on callow, lumpish, and selfish youth peril, sorrow, and the shadow of death can bestow dignity, and even sometimes wisdom.

[1] Preface to the *Lilac Fairy Book*.

Let us not divide the human race into Eloi and Morlocks pretty children – 'elves' as the eighteenth century often idiotically called them – with their fairy-tales (carefully pruned), and dark Morlocks tending their machines. If fairy-story as a kind is worth reading at all it is worthy to be written for and read by adults. They will, of course, put more in and get more out than children can. Then, as a branch of a genuine art, children may hope to get fairy-stories fit for them to read and yet within their measure; as they may hope to get suitable introductions to poetry, history, and the sciences. Though it may be better for them to read some things, especially fairy-stories, that are beyond their measure rather than short of it. Their books like their clothes should allow for growth, and their books at any rate should encourage it.

Very well, then. If adults are to read fairy-stories as a natural branch of literature – neither playing at being children, nor pretending to be choosing for children, nor being boys who would not grow up – what are the values and functions of this kind? That is, I think, the last and most important question. I have already hinted at some of my answers. First of all: if written with art, the prime value of fairy-stories will simply be that value which, as literature, they share with other literary forms. But fairy-stories offer also, in a peculiar degree or mode, these things: Fantasy, Recovery, Escape, Consolation, all things of which children have, as a rule, less need than older people. Most of them are nowadays very commonly considered to be bad for anybody. I will consider them briefly, and will begin with *Fantasy*.

FANTASY

The human mind is capable of forming mental images of things not actually present. The faculty of conceiving the images is (or was) naturally called Imagination. But in recent times, in technical not normal language, Imagination has often been held to be something higher than the mere image-making, ascribed to the operations of Fancy (a reduced and depreciatory form of the older word Fantasy); an attempt is thus made to restrict, I should say misapply, Imagination to 'the power of giving to ideal creations the inner consistency of reality'.

Ridiculous though it may be for one so ill-instructed to have an opinion on this critical matter, I venture to think the verbal distinction philologically inappropriate, and the analysis inaccurate. The mental power of image-making is one thing, or aspect; and it should appropriately be called Imagination. The perception of the image, the grasp of its implications, and the control, which are necessary to a successful expression, may vary in vividness and strength: but this is a difference of degree in Imagination, not a difference in kind. The achievement of the expression, which gives (or seems to give) 'the inner consistency of reality',[1] is indeed another thing, or aspect, needing another name: Art, the operative link between Imagination and the final result, Sub-creation. For my present purpose I require a word which shall embrace both the Sub-creative Art in itself and a quality of strangeness and wonder in the Expression, derived from the Image: a quality essential to fairy-story. I propose, therefore, to arrogate to myself the powers of Humpty-Dumpty, and to use Fantasy for this purpose: in a sense, that is, which

[1] That is: which commands or induces Secondary Belief.

combines with its older and higher use as an equivalent of Imagination the derived notions of 'unreality' (that is, of unlikeness to the Primary World), of freedom from the domination of observed 'fact', in short of the fantastic. I am thus not only aware but glad of the etymological and semantic connections of *fantasy* with *fantastic*: with images of things that are not only 'not actually present', but which are indeed not to be found in our primary world at all, or are generally believed not to be found there. But while admitting that, I do not assent to the depreciative tone. That the images are of things not in the primary world (if that indeed is possible) is a virtue not a vice. Fantasy (in this sense) is, I think, not a lower but a higher form of Art, indeed the most nearly pure form, and so (when achieved) the most potent.

Fantasy, of course, starts out with an advantage: arresting strangeness. But that advantage has been turned against it, and has contributed to its disrepute. Many people dislike being 'arrested'. They dislike any meddling with the Primary World, or such small glimpses of it as are familiar to them. They, therefore, stupidly and even maliciously confound Fantasy with Dreaming, in which there is no Art;[1] and with mental disorders, in which there is not even control: with delusion and hallucination.

But the error or malice, engendered by disquiet and consequent dislike, is not the only cause of this confusion. Fantasy has also an essential drawback: it is difficult to achieve. Fantasy may be, as I think, not less but more subcreative; but at any rate it is found in practice that 'the inner consistency of reality' is more difficult to produce, the more

[1] This is not true of all dreams. In some Fantasy seems to take a part. But this is exceptional. Fantasy is a rational not an irrational activity.

unlike are the images and the rearrangements of primary material to the actual arrangements of the Primary World. It is easier to produce this kind of 'reality' with more 'sober' material. Fantasy thus, too often, remains undeveloped; it is and has been used frivolously, or only half-seriously, or merely for decoration: it remains merely 'fanciful'. Anyone inheriting the fantastic device of human language can say *the green sun*. Many can then imagine or picture it. But that is not enough – though it may already be a more potent thing than many a 'thumbnail sketch' or 'transcript of life' that receives literary praise.

To make a Secondary World inside which the green sun will be credible, commanding Secondary Belief, will probably require labour and thought, and will certainly demand a special skill, a kind of elvish craft. Few attempt such difficult tasks. But when they are attempted and in any degree accomplished then we have a rare achievement of Art: indeed narrative art, story-making in its primary and most potent mode.

In human art Fantasy is a thing best left to words, to true literature. In painting, for instance, the visible presentation of the fantastic image is technically too easy; the hand tends to outrun the mind, even to overthrow it.[1] Silliness or morbidity are frequent results. It is a misfortune that Drama, an art fundamentally distinct from Literature, should so commonly be considered together with it, or as a branch of it. Among these misfortunes we may reckon the depreciation of Fantasy. For in part at least this depreciation is due to the natural desire of critics to cry up the forms of literature or 'imagination' that they themselves, innately or by training, prefer. And criticism in a country that has produced so great a Drama, and possesses the works of William Shakespeare,

[1] See Note E at end (p. 76).

tends to be far too dramatic. But Drama is naturally hostile to Fantasy. Fantasy, even of the simplest kind, hardly ever succeeds in Drama, when that is presented as it should be, visibly and audibly acted. Fantastic forms are not to be counterfeited. Men dressed up as talking animals may achieve buffoonery or mimicry, but they do not achieve Fantasy. This is, I think, well illustrated by the failure of the bastard form, pantomime. The nearer it is to 'dramatised fairy-story' the worse it is. It is only tolerable when the plot and its fantasy are reduced to a mere vestigiary framework for farce, and no 'belief' of any kind in any part of the performance is required or expected of anybody. This is, of course, partly due to the fact that the producers of drama have to, or try to, work with mechanism to represent either Fantasy or Magic. I once saw a so-called 'children's panto-mime', the straight story of *Puss-in-Boots*, with even the metamorphosis of the ogre into a mouse. Had this been mechanically successful it would either have terrified the spectators or else have been just a turn of high-class conjur-ing. As it was, though done with some ingenuity of lighting, disbelief had not so much to be suspended as hung, drawn, and quartered.

In *Macbeth*, when it is read, I find the witches tolerable: they have a narrative function and some hint of dark signifi-cance; though they are vulgarised, poor things of their kind. They are almost intolerable in the play. They would be quite intolerable, if I were not fortified by some memory of them as they are in the story as read. I am told that I should feel differently if I had the mind of the period, with its witch-hunts and witch-trials. But that is to say: if I regarded the witches as possible, indeed likely, in the Primary World; in other words, if they ceased to be 'Fantasy'. That argument concedes the point. To be dissolved, or to be degraded, is the likely fate of Fantasy when a dramatist tries to use it, even such a dramatist as Shakespeare. *Macbeth* is indeed a work by a playwright who ought, at least on this occasion, to have written a story, if he had the skill or patience for that art.

A reason, more important, I think, than the inadequacy of stage-effects, is this: Drama has, of its very nature, already attempted a kind of bogus, or shall I say at least substitute, magic: *the visible and audible presentation of imaginary men in a story*. That is in itself an attempt to counterfeit the magician's wand. To introduce, even with mechanical success, into this quasi-magical secondary world a further fantasy or magic is to demand, as it were, an inner or tertiary world. It is a world too much. To make such a thing may not be impossible. I have never seen it done with success. But at least it cannot be claimed as the proper mode of drama, in which walking and talking people have been found to be the natural instruments of Art and illusion.[1]

For this precise reason – that the characters, and even the scenes, are in Drama not imagined but actually beheld – Drama is, even though it uses a similar material (words, verse, plot), an art fundamentally different from narrative art. Thus, if you prefer Drama to Literature (as many literary critics plainly do), or form your critical theories primarily from dramatic critics, or even from Drama, you are apt to misunderstand pure story-making, and to constrain it to the limitations of stage-plays. You are, for instance, likely to prefer characters, even the basest and dullest, to things. Very little about trees as trees can be got into a play.

Now 'Faërian Drama' – those plays which according to abundant records the elves have often presented to men – can produce Fantasy with a realism and immediacy beyond the

[1] See Note F at end (p. 77).

compass of any human mechanism. As a result their usual effect (upon a man) is to go beyond Secondary Belief. If you are present at a Faërian drama you yourself are, or think that you are, bodily inside its Secondary World. The experience may be very similar to Dreaming and has (it would seem) sometimes (by men) been confounded with it. But in Faërian drama you are in a dream that some other mind is weaving, and the knowledge of that alarming fact may slip from your grasp. To experience *directly* a Secondary World: the potion is too strong, and you give to it Primary Belief, however marvellous the events. You are deluded – whether that is the intention of the elves (always or at any time) is another question. They at any rate are not themselves deluded. This is for them a form of Art, and distinct from Wizardry or Magic, properly so called. They do not live in it, though they can, perhaps, afford to spend more time at it than human artists can. The Primary World, Reality, of elves and men is the same, if differently valued and perceived.

We need a word for this elvish craft, but all the words that have been applied to it have been blurred and confused with other things. Magic is ready to hand, and I have used it above (p. 17), but I should not have done so: Magic should be reserved for the operations of the Magician. Art is the human process that produces by the way (it is not its only or ultimate object) Secondary Belief. Art of the same sort, if more skilled and effortless, the elves can also use, or so the reports seem to show; but the more potent and specially elvish craft I will, for lack of a less debatable word, call Enchantment. Enchantment produces a Secondary World into which both designer and spectator can enter, to the satisfaction of their senses while they are inside; but in its purity it is artistic in desire and purpose. Magic produces, or pretends to produce, an alteration in the Primary World. It does not matter by whom it is said to be practised, fay or mortal, it remains distinct from the other two; it is not an art but a technique; its desire is *power* in this world, domination of things and wills.

To the elvish craft, Enchantment, Fantasy aspires, and when it is successful of all forms of human art most nearly approaches. At the heart of many man-made stories of the elves lies, open or concealed, pure or alloyed, the desire for a living, realised sub-creative art, which (however much it may outwardly resemble it) is inwardly wholly different from the greed for self-centred power which is the mark of the mere Magician. Of this desire the elves, in their better (but still perilous) part, are largely made; and it is from them that we may learn what is the central desire and aspiration of human Fantasy – even if the elves are, all the more in so far as they are, only a product of Fantasy itself. That creative desire is only cheated by counterfeits, whether the innocent but clumsy devices of the human dramatist, or the malevolent frauds of the magicians. In this world it is for men unsatisfiable, and so imperishable. Uncorrupted it does not seek delusion, nor bewitchment and domination; it seeks shared enrichment, partners in making and delight, not slaves.

To many, Fantasy, this sub-creative art which plays strange tricks with the world and all that is in it, combining nouns and redistributing adjectives, has seemed suspect, if not illegitimate. To some it has seemed at least a childish folly, a thing only for peoples or for persons in their youth. As for its legitimacy I will say no more than to quote a brief passage from a letter I once wrote to a man who described myth and fairy-story as 'lies'; though to do him justice he was kind enough and confused enough to call fairy-story making 'Breathing a lie through Silver'.

'Dear Sir,' I said – 'Although now long estranged,
Man is not wholly lost nor wholly changed.
Dis-graced he may be, yet is not de-throned,
and keeps the rags of lordship once he owned:
Man, Sub-creator, the refracted Light
through whom is splintered from a single White
to many hues, and endlessly combined
in living shapes that move from mind to mind.
Though all the crannies of the world we filled
with Elves and Goblins, though we dared to build
Gods and their houses out of dark and light,
and sowed the seed of dragons – 'twas our right
(used or misused). That right has not decayed:
we make still by the law in which we're made.'

Fantasy is a natural human activity. It certainly does not destroy or even insult Reason; and it does not either blunt the appetite for, nor obscure the perception of, scientific verity. On the contrary. The keener and the clearer is the reason, the better fantasy will it make. If men were ever in a state in which they did not want to know or could not perceive truth (facts or evidence), then Fantasy would languish until they were cured. If they ever get into that state (it would not seem at all impossible), Fantasy will perish, and become Morbid Delusion.

For creative Fantasy is founded upon the hard recognition that things are so in the world as it appears under the sun; on a recognition of fact, but not a slavery to it. So upon logic was founded the nonsense that displays itself in the tales and rhymes of Lewis Carroll. If men really could not distinguish between frogs and men, fairy-stories about frog-kings would not have arisen.

Fantasy can, of course, be carried to excess. It can be ill done. It can be put to evil uses. It may even delude the minds out of which it came. But of what human thing in this fallen world is that not true ? Men have conceived not only of elves, but they have imagined gods, and worshipped them, even worshipped those most deformed by their authors' own evil. But they have made false gods out of other materials: their notions, their banners, their monies; even their sciences and their social and economic theories have demanded human sacrifice. *Abusus non tollit usum.* Fantasy remains a human right: we make in our measure and in our derivative mode, because we are made: and not only made, but made in the image and likeness of a Maker.

RECOVERY, ESCAPE, CONSOLATION

As for old age, whether personal or belonging to the times in which we live, it may be true, as is often supposed, that this imposes disabilities (cf. p. 40). But it is in the main an idea produced by the mere *study* of fairy-stories. The analytic study of fairy-stories is as bad a preparation for the enjoying or the writing of them as would be the historical study of the drama of all lands and times for the enjoyment or writing of stage-plays. The study may indeed become depressing. It is easy for the student to feel that with all his labour he is collecting only a few leaves, many of them now torn or decayed, from the countless foliage of the Tree of Tales, with which the Forest of Days is carpeted. It seems vain to add to the litter. Who can design a new leaf? The patterns from bud to unfolding, and the colours from spring to autumn were all discovered by men long ago. But that is not true. The seed of the tree can be replanted in almost any soil, even in one so smoke-ridden (as Lang said) as that of England. Spring is, of course, not really less beautiful because we have seen or heard of other like events: like events, never from world's beginning to world's end the same event. Each leaf, of oak and ash and thorn, is a unique embodiment of the pattern, and for some this very year may be *the* embodiment, the first ever seen and recognised, though oaks have put forth leaves for countless generations of men.

We do not, or need not, despair of drawing because all lines must be either curved or straight, nor of painting because there are only three 'primary' colours. We may indeed be older now, in so far as we are heirs in enjoyment or in practice of many generations of ancestors in the arts. In this inheritance of wealth there may be a danger of boredom or of anxiety to be original, and that may lead to a distaste for fine drawing, delicate pattern, and 'pretty' colours, or else to mere manipulation and over-elaboration of old material, clever and heartless. But the true road of escape from such weariness is not to be found in the wilfully awkward, clumsy, or misshapen, not in making all things dark or unremittingly violent; nor in the mixing of colours on through subtlety to drabness, and the fantastical complication of shapes to the point of silliness and on towards delirium. Before we reach such states we need recovery. We should look at green again, and be startled anew (but not blinded) by blue and yellow and red. We should meet the centaur and the dragon, and then perhaps suddenly behold, like the ancient shepherds, sheep, and dogs, and horses – and wolves. This recovery fairy-stories help us to make. In that sense only a taste for them may make us, or keep us, childish.

Recovery (which includes return and renewal of health) is a re-gaining – regaining of a clear view. I do not say 'seeing things as they are' and involve myself with the philosophers, though I might venture to say 'seeing things as we are (or were) meant to see them' – as things apart from ourselves.

We need, in any case, to clean our windows; so that the things seen clearly may be freed from the drab blur of triteness or familiarity – from possessiveness. Of all faces those of our *familiares* are the ones both most difficult to play fantastic tricks with, and most difficult really to see with fresh attention, perceiving their likeness and unlikeness: that they are faces, and yet unique faces. This triteness is really the penalty of 'appropriation': the things that are trite, or (in a bad sense) familiar, are the things that we have appropriated, legally or mentally. We say we know them. They have become like the things which once attracted us by their glitter, or their colour, or their shape, and we laid hands on them, and then locked them in our hoard, acquired them, and acquiring ceased to look at them.

Of course, fairy-stories are not the only means of recovery, or prophylactic against loss. Humility is enough. And there is (especially for the humble) *Mooreeffoc*, or Chestertonian Fantasy. *Mooreeffoc* is a fantastic word, but it could be seen written up in every town in this land. It is Coffee-room, viewed from the inside through a glass door, as it was seen by Dickens on a dark London day; and it was used by Chesterton to denote the queerness of things that have become trite, when they are seen suddenly from a new angle. That kind of 'fantasy' most people would allow to be wholesome enough; and it can never lack for material. But it has, I think, only a limited power; for the reason that recovery of freshness of vision is its only virtue. The word *Mooreeffoc* may cause you suddenly to realise that England is an utterly alien land, lost either in some remote past age glimpsed by history, or in some strange dim future to be reached only by a time-machine; to see the amazing oddity and interest of its inhabitants and their customs and feeding-habits; but it cannot do more than that: act as a time-telescope focused on one spot. Creative fantasy, because it is mainly trying to do something else (make something new), may open your hoard and let all the locked things fly away like cage-birds. The gems all turn into flowers or flames, and you will be warned that all you had (or knew) was dangerous and potent, not really effectively chained, free and wild; no more yours than they were you.

The 'fantastic' elements in verse and prose of other kinds, even when only decorative or occasional, help in this release. But not so thoroughly as a fairy-story, a thing built on or about Fantasy, of which Fantasy is the core. Fantasy is made out of the Primary World, but a good craftsman loves his material, and has a knowledge and feeling for clay, stone and wood which only the art of making can give. By the forging of Gram cold iron was revealed; by the making of Pegasus horses were ennobled; in the Trees of the Sun and Moon root and stock, flower and fruit are manifested in glory.

And actually fairy-stories deal largely, or (the better ones) mainly, with simple or fundamental things, untouched by Fantasy, but these simplicities are made all the more luminous by their setting. For the story-maker who allows himself to be 'free with' Nature can be her lover not her slave. It was in fairy-stories that I first divined the potency of the words, and the wonder of the things, such as stone, and wood, and iron; tree and grass; house and fire; bread and wine.

I will now conclude by considering Escape and Consolation, which are naturally closely connected. Though fairy-stories are of course by no means the only medium of Escape, they are today one of the most obvious and (to some) outrageous forms of 'escapist' literature; and it is thus reasonable to attach to a consideration of them some considerations of this term 'escape' in criticism generally.

I have claimed that Escape is one of the main functions of

fairy-stories, and since I do not disapprove of them, it is plain that I do not accept the tone of scorn or pity with which 'Escape' is now so often used: a tone for which the uses of the word outside literary criticism give no warrant at all. In what the misusers are fond of calling Real Life, Escape is evidently as a rule very practical, and may even be heroic. In real life it is difficult to blame it, unless it fails; in criticism it would seem to be the worse the better it succeeds. Evidently we are faced by a misuse of words, and also by a confusion of thought. Why should a man be scorned, if, finding himself in prison, he tries to get out and go home? Or if, when he cannot do so, he thinks and talks about other topics than jailers and prison-walls? The world outside has not become less real because the prisoner cannot see it. In using Escape in this way the critics have chosen the wrong word, and, what is more, they are confusing, not always by sincere error, the Escape of the Prisoner with the Flight of the Deserter. Just so a Party-spokesman might have labelled departure from the misery of the Führer's or any other Reich and even criticism of it as treachery. In the same way these critics, to make confusion worse, and so to bring into contempt their opponents, stick their label of scorn not only on to Desertion, but on to real Escape, and what are often its companions, Disgust, Anger, Condemnation, and Revolt. Not only do they confound the escape of the prisoner with the flight of the deserter; but they would seem to prefer the acquiescence of the 'quisling' to the resistance of the patriot. To such thinking you have only to say 'the land you loved is doomed' to excuse any treachery, indeed to glorify it.

For a trifling instance: not to mention (indeed not to parade) electric street-lamps of mass-produced pattern in your tale is Escape (in that sense). But it may, almost certainly does, proceed from a considered disgust for so typical a product of the Robot Age, that combines elaboration and ingenuity of means with ugliness, and (often) with inferiority of result. These lamps may be excluded from the tale simply because they are bad lamps; and it is possible that one of the lessons to be learnt from the story is the realisation of this fact. But out comes the big stick: 'Electric lamps have come to stay', they say. Long ago Chesterton truly remarked that, as soon as he heard that anything 'had come to stay', he knew that it would be very soon replaced – indeed regarded as pitiably obsolete and shabby. 'The march of Science, its tempo quickened by the needs of war, goes inexorably on . . . making some things obsolete, and foreshadowing new developments in the utilisation of electricity': an advertisement. This says the same thing only more menacingly. The electric street-lamp may indeed be ignored, simply because it is so insignificant and transient. Fairy-stories, at any rate, have many more permanent and fundamental things to talk about. Lightning, for example. The escapist is not so subservient to the whims of evanescent fashion as these opponents. He does not make things (which it may be quite rational to regard as bad) his masters or his gods by worshipping them as inevitable, even 'inexorable'. And his opponents, so easily contemptuous, have no guarantee that he will stop there: he might rouse men to pull down the street-lamps. Escapism has another and even wickeder face: Reaction.

Not long ago – incredible though it may seem – I heard a clerk of Oxford declare that he 'welcomed' the proximity of mass-production robot factories, and the roar of self-obstructive mechanical traffic, because it brought his university into 'contact with real life'. He may have meant that the way men were living and working in the twentieth century was increasing in barbarity at an alarming rate, and that the loud demonstration of this in the streets of Oxford might serve as a warning that it is not possible to preserve for long an oasis of sanity in a desert of unreason by mere fences, without actual offensive action (practical and intellectual). I fear he did not. In any case the expression 'real life' in this context seems to fall short of academic standards. The notion that motor-cars are more 'alive' than, say, centaurs or dragons is curious; that they are more 'real' than, say, horses is pathetically absurd. How real, how startlingly alive is a factory chimney compared with an elm tree: poor obsolete thing, insubstantial dream of an escapist!

For my part, I cannot convince myself that the roof of Bletchley station is more 'real' than the clouds. And as an artefact I find it less inspiring than the legendary dome of heaven. The bridge to platform 4 is to me less interesting than Bifröst guarded by Heimdall with the Gjallarhorn. From the wildness of my heart I cannot exclude the question whether railway-engineers, if they had been brought up on more fantasy, might not have done better with all their abundant means than they commonly do. Fairy-stories might be, I guess, better Masters of Arts than the academic person I have referred to.

Much that he (I must suppose) and others (certainly) would call 'serious' literature is no more than play under a glass roof by the side of a municipal swimming-bath. Fairy-stories may invent monsters that fly the air or dwell in the deep, but at least they do not try to escape from heaven or the sea.

And if we leave aside for a moment 'fantasy', I do not think that the reader or the maker of fairy-stories need even be ashamed of the 'escape' of archaism: of preferring not dragons but horses, castles, sailing-ships, bows and arrows; not only elves, but knights and kings and priests. For it is after all possible for a rational man, after reflection (quite unconnected with fairy-story or romance), to arrive at the condemnation, implicit at least in the mere silence of 'escapist' literature, of progressive things like factories, or the machine-guns and bombs that appear to be their most natural and inevitable, dare we say 'inexorable', products.

'The rawness and ugliness of modern European life' – that real life whose contact we should welcome – 'is the sign of a biological inferiority, of an insufficient or false reaction to environment.'[1] The maddest castle that ever came out of a giant's bag in a wild Gaelic story is not only much less ugly than a robot-factory, it is also (to use a very modern phrase) 'in a very real sense' a great deal more real. Why should we not escape from or condemn the 'grim Assyrian' absurdity of top-hats, or the Morlockian horror of factories ? They are condemned even by the writers of that most escapist form of all literature, stories of Science fiction. These prophets often foretell (and many seem to yearn for) a world like one big glass-roofed railway-station. But from them it is as a rule very hard to gather what men in such a world-town will *do*. They may abandon the 'full Victorian panoply' for loose garments (with zip-fasteners), but will use this freedom mainly, it would appear, in order to play with mechanical toys in the soon-cloying game of moving at high speed. To judge by some of these tales they will still be as lustful,

[1] Christopher Dawson, *Progress and Religion*, pp. 58, 59. Later he adds: 'The full Victorian panoply of top-hat and frock-coat was undoubtedly expressed essential in the nineteenth-century culture, and hence it has with that culture spread all over the world, as no fashion of clothing has ever done before. It is possible that our descendants will recognise in it a kind of grim Assyrian beauty, fit emblem of the ruthless and great age that created it; but however that may be, it misses the direct and inevitable beauty that all clothing should have, because like its parent culture it was out of touch with the life of nature and of human nature as well.'

vengeful, and greedy as ever; and the ideals of their idealists hardly reach farther than the splendid notion of building more towns of the same sort on other planets. It is indeed an age of 'improved means to deteriorated ends'. It is part of the essential malady of such days – producing the desire to escape, not indeed from life, but from our present time and self-made misery – that we are acutely conscious both of the ugliness of our works, and of their evil. So that to us evil and ugliness seem indissolubly allied. We find it difficult to conceive of evil and beauty together. The fear of the beautiful fay that ran through the elder ages almost eludes our grasp. Even more alarming: goodness is itself bereft of its proper beauty. In Faërie one can indeed conceive of an ogre who possesses a castle hideous as a nightmare (for the evil of the ogre wills it so), but one cannot conceive of a house built with a good purpose – an inn, a hostel for travellers, the hall of a virtuous and noble king – that is yet sickeningly ugly. At the present day it would be rash to hope to see one that was not – unless it was built before our time.

This, however, is the modern and special (or accidental) 'escapist' aspect of fairy-stories, which they share with romances and other stories out of or about the past. Many stories out of the past have only become 'escapist' in their appeal through surviving from a time when men were as a rule delighted with the work of their hands into our time, when many men feel disgust with man-made things.

But there are also other and more profound 'escapisms' that have always appeared in fairy-tale and legend. There are other things more grim and terrible to fly from than the noise, stench, ruthlessness, and extravagance of the internal-combustion engine. There are hunger, thirst, poverty, pain, sorrow, injustice, death. And even when men are not facing hard things such as these, there are ancient limitations from which fairy-stories offer a sort of escape, and old ambitions and desires (touching the very roots of fantasy) to which they offer a kind of satisfaction and consolation. Some are pardonable weaknesses or curiosities: such as the desire to visit, free as a fish, the deep sea; or the longing for the noiseless, gracious, economical flight of a bird, that longing which the aeroplane cheats, except in rare moments, seen high and by wind and distance noiseless, turning in the sun: that is, precisely when imagined and not used. There are profounder wishes: such as the desire to converse with other living things. On this desire, as ancient as the Fall, is largely founded the talking of beasts and creatures in fairy-tales, and especially the magical understanding of their proper speech. This is the root, and not the 'confusion' attributed to the minds of men of the unrecorded past, an alleged 'absence of the sense of separation of ourselves from beasts'.[1] A vivid sense of that separation is very ancient; but also a sense that it was a severance: a strange fate and a guilt lies on us. Other creatures are like other realms with which Man has broken off relations, and sees now only from the outside at a distance, being at war with them, or on the terms of an uneasy armistice. There are a few men who are privileged to travel abroad a little; others must be content with travellers' tales. Even about frogs. In speaking of that rather odd but widespread fairy-story *The Frog King* Max Müller asked in his prim way: 'How came such a story ever to be invented? Human beings were, we may hope, at all times sufficiently enlightened to know that a marriage between a frog and the daughter of a queen was absurd.' Indeed we may hope so! For if not, there would be no point in this story at all, depending as it does essentially on the sense of the absurdity. Folk-lore origins (or guesses about them) are here quite

[1] See Note G at end (p. 78).

beside the point. It is of little avail to consider totemism. For certainly whatever customs or beliefs about frogs and wells lie behind this story, the frog-shape was and is preserved in the fairy-story[1] precisely because it was so queer and the marriage absurd, indeed abominable. Though, of course, in the versions which concern us, Gaelic, German, English,[2] there is in fact no wedding between a princess and a frog: the frog was an enchanted prince. And the point of the story lies not in thinking frogs possible mates, but in the necessity of keeping promises (even those with intolerable consequences) that, together with observing prohibitions, runs through all Fairyland. This is one of the notes of the horns of Elfland, and not a dim note.

And lastly there is the oldest and deepest desire, the Great Escape: the Escape from Death. Fairy-stories provide many examples and modes of this – which might be called the genuine *escapist*, or (I would say) *fugitive* spirit. But so do other stories (notably those of scientific inspiration), and so do other studies. Fairy-stories are made by men not by fairies. The human stories of the elves are doubtless full of the Escape from Deathlessness. But our stories cannot be expected always to rise above our common level. They often do. Few lessons are taught more clearly in them than the burden of that kind of immortality, or rather endless serial living, to which the 'fugitive' would fly. For the fairy-story is specially apt to teach such things, of old and still today. Death is the theme that most inspired George MacDonald.

But the 'consolation' of fairy-tales has another aspect than the imaginative satisfaction of ancient desires. Far more important is the Consolation of the Happy Ending. Almost

---

[1] Or group of similar stories.

[2] *The Queen who sought drink from a certain Well and the Lorgann* (Campbell, xxiii); *Der Froschkönig*; *The Maid and the Frog*.

I would venture to assert that all complete fairy-stories must have it. At least I would say that Tragedy is the true form of Drama, its highest function; but the opposite is true of Fairy-story. Since we do not appear to possess a word that expresses this opposite – I will call it *Eucatastrophe*. The *eucatastrophic* tale is the true form of fairy-tale, and its highest function.

The consolation of fairy-stories, the joy of the happy ending: or more correctly of the good catastrophe, the sudden joyous 'turn' (for there is no true end to any fairy-tale):[1] this joy, which is one of the things which fairy-stories can produce supremely well, is not essentially 'escapist', nor 'fugitive'. In its fairy-tale – or otherworld – setting, it is a sudden and miraculous grace: never to be counted on to recur. It does not deny the existence of *dyscatastrophe*, of sorrow and failure: the possibility of these is necessary to the joy of deliverance; it denies (in the face of much evidence, if you will) universal final defeat and in so far is *evangelium*, giving a fleeting glimpse of Joy, Joy beyond the walls of the world, poignant as grief.

It is the mark of a good fairy-story, of the higher or more complete kind, that however wild its events, however fantastic or terrible the adventures, it can give to child or man that hears it, when the 'turn' comes, a catch of the breath, a beat and lifting of the heart, near to (or indeed accompanied by) tears, as keen as that given by any form of literary art, and having a peculiar quality.

Even modern fairy-stories can produce this effect sometimes. It is not an easy thing to do; it depends on the whole story which is the setting of the turn, and yet it reflects a glory backwards. A tale that in any measure succeeds in this point has not wholly failed, whatever flaws it may possess,

[1] See Note H at end (p. 78).

and whatever mixture or confusion of purpose. It happens even in Andrew Lang's own fairy-story, *Prince Prigio*, unsatisfactory in many ways as that is. When 'each knight came alive and lifted his sword and shouted "long live Prince Prigio" ', the joy has a little of that strange mythical fairy-story quality, greater than the event described. It would have none in Lang's tale, if the event described were not a piece of more serious fairy-story 'fantasy' than the main bulk of the story, which is in general more frivolous, having the half-mocking smile of the courtly, sophisticated *Conte*.[1] Far more powerful and poignant is the effect in a serious tale of Faërie.[2] In such stories when the sudden 'turn' comes we get a piercing glimpse of joy, and heart's desire, that for a moment passes outside the frame, rends indeed the very web of story, and lets a gleam come through.

> Seven long years I served for thee,
> The glassy hill I clamb for thee,
> The bluidy shirt I wrang for thee,
> And wilt thou not wauken and turn to me?

He heard and turned to her.[3]

---

[1] This is characteristic of Lang's wavering balance. On the surface the story is a follower of the 'courtly' French *conte* with a satirical twist, and of Thackeray's *Rose and the Ring* in particular – a kind which being superficial, even frivolous, by nature, does not produce or aim at producing anything so profound; but underneath lies the deeper spirit of the romantic Lang.

[2] Of the kind which Lang called 'traditional', and really preferred.

[3] *The Black Bull of Norroway.*

EPILOGUE

This 'joy' which I have selected as the mark of the true fairy-story (or romance), or as the seal upon it, merits more consideration.

Probably every writer making a secondary world, a fantasy, every sub-creator, wishes in some measure to be a real maker, or hopes that he is drawing on reality: hopes that the peculiar quality of this secondary world (if not all the details)[1] are derived from Reality, or are flowing into it. If he indeed achieves a quality that can fairly be described by the dictionary definition: 'inner consistency of reality', it is difficult to conceive how this can be, if the work does not in some way partake of reality. The peculiar quality of the 'joy' in successful Fantasy can thus be explained as a sudden glimpse of the underlying reality or truth. It is not only a 'consolation' for the sorrow of this world, but a satisfaction, and an answer to that question, 'Is it true?' The answer to this question that I gave at first was (quite rightly): 'If you have built your little world well, yes: it is true in that world'. That is enough for the artist (or the artist part of the artist). But in the 'eucatastrophe' we see in a brief vision that the answer may be greater – it may be a far-off gleam or echo of *evangelium* in the real world. The use of this word gives a hint of my epilogue. It is a serious and dangerous matter. It is presumptuous of me to touch upon such a theme; but if by grace what I say has in any respect any validity, it is, of course, only one facet of a truth incalculably rich: finite only because the capacity of Man for whom this was done is finite.

[1] For all details may not be 'true': it is seldom that the 'inspiration' is so strong and lasting that it leavens all the lump, and does not leave much that is mere uninspired 'invention'.

I would venture to say that approaching the Christian Story from this direction, it has long been my feeling (a joyous feeling) that God redeemed the corrupt making-creatures, men, in a way fitting to this aspect, as to others, of their strange nature. The Gospels contain a fairy-story, or a story of a larger kind which embraces all the essence of fairy-stories. They contain many marvels – peculiarly artistic,[1] beautiful, and moving: 'mythical' in their perfect, self-contained significance; and among the marvels is the greatest and most complete conceivable eucatastrophe. But this story has entered History and the primary world; the desire and aspiration of sub-creation has been raised to the fulfilment of Creation. The Birth of Christ is the eucatastrophe of Man's history. The Resurrection is the eucatastrophe of the story of the Incarnation. This story begins and ends in joy. It has pre-eminently the 'inner consistency of reality'. There is no tale ever told that men would rather find was true, and none which so many sceptical men have accepted as true on its own merits. For the Art of it has the supremely convincing tone of Primary Art, that is, of Creation. To reject it leads either to sadness or to wrath.

It is not difficult to imagine the peculiar excitement and joy that one would feel, if any specially beautiful fairy-story were found to be 'primarily' true, its narrative to be history, without thereby necessarily losing the mythical or allegorical significance that it had possessed. It is not difficult, for one is not called upon to try and conceive anything of a quality unknown. The joy would have exactly the same quality, if not the same degree, as the joy which the 'turn' in a fairy-story gives: such joy has the very taste of primary truth. (Otherwise its name would not be joy.) It looks forward (or

[1] The Art is here in the story itself rather than in the telling; for the Author of the story was not the evangelists.

backward: the direction in this regard is unimportant) to the Great Eucatastrophe. The Christian joy, the *Gloria*, is of the same kind; but it is pre-eminently (infinitely, if our capacity were not finite) high and joyous. But this story is supreme; and it is true. Art has been verified. God is the Lord, of angels, and of men – and of elves. Legend and History have met and fused.

But in God's kingdom the presence of the greatest does not depress the small. Redeemed Man is still man. Story, fantasy, still go on, and should go on. The Evangelium has not abrogated legends; it has hallowed them, especially the 'happy ending'. The Christian has still to work, with mind as well as body, to suffer, hope, and die; but he may now perceive that all his bents and faculties have a purpose, which can be redeemed. So great is the bounty with which he has been treated that he may now, perhaps, fairly dare to guess that in Fantasy he may actually assist in the effoliation and multiple enrichment of creation. All tales may come true; and yet, at the last, redeemed, they may be as like and as unlike the forms that we give them as Man, finally redeemed, will be like and unlike the fallen that we know.

NOTES

A (p. 21)

The very root (not only the use) of their 'marvels' is satiric, a mockery of unreason; and the 'dream' element is not a mere machinery of introduction and ending, but inherent in the action and transitions. These things children can perceive and appreci-ate, if left to themselves. But to many, as it was to me, *Alice* is presented as a fairy-story and while this misunderstanding lasts, the distaste for the dream-machinery is felt. There is no suggestion of dream in *The Wind in the Willows*. 'The Mole had been working very hard all the morning, spring-cleaning his little house.' So it begins, and that correct tone is maintained. It is all the more remarkable that A. A. Milne, so great an admirer of this excellent book, should have prefaced to his dramatised version a 'whimsical' opening in which a child is seen telephoning with a daffodil. Or perhaps it is not very remarkable, for a perceptive admirer (as distinct from a great admirer) of the book would never have attempted to dramatise it. Naturally only the simpler ingredients, the pantomime, and the satiric beast-fable elements, are capable of presentation in this form. The play is, on the lower level of drama, tolerably good fun, especially for those who have not read the book; but some children that I took to see *Toad of Toad Hall* brought away as their chief memory nausea at the opening. For the rest they preferred their recollections of the book.

B (p. 37)

Of course, these details, as a rule, got into the tales, *even in the days when they were real practices*, because they had a story-making value. If I were to write a story in which it happened that a man was hanged, that *might* show in later ages, if the story survived – in itself a sign that the story possessed some permanent, and more than local or temporary, value – that it was written at a period when men were really hanged, as a legal practice. *Might*: the inference would not, of course, in that future time be certain. For certainty on that point the future inquirer would have to know definitely when hanging was practised and when I lived. I could have borrowed the incident from other times and places, from other stories; I could simply have invented it. But even if this inference happened to be correct, the hanging-scene would only occur in the story, (*a*) because I was aware of the dramatic, tragic, or macabre force of this incident in my tale, and (*b*) because those who handed it down felt this force enough to make them keep the incident in. Distance of time, sheer antiquity and alienness, might later sharpen the edge of the tragedy or the horror; but the edge must be there even for the elvish hone of antiquity to whet it. The least useful question, therefore, for literary critics at any rate, to ask or to answer about Iphigeneia, daughter of Agamemnon, is: Does the legend of her sacrifice at Aulis come down from a time when human-sacrifice was commonly practised?

I say only 'as a rule', because it is conceivable that what is now regarded as a 'story' was once something different in intent: e.g. a record of fact or ritual. I mean 'record' strictly. A story invented to explain a ritual (a process that is sometimes supposed to have frequently occurred) remains primarily a story. It takes form as such, and will survive (long after the ritual evidently) only because of its story-values. In some cases details that now are notable merely because they are strange may have once been so everyday and unregarded that they were slipped in casually: like mentioning that a man 'raised his hat', or 'caught a train'. But such casual details will not long survive change in everyday habits. Not in a period of oral transmission. In a period of writing (and of rapid changes in habits) a story may remain unchanged long enough for even its casual details to acquire the value of quaintness or queerness. Much of Dickens now has this air. One can open today an edition of a novel of his that was bought and first read when things were so in everyday life as they are in the story, though these everyday details are now already as remote from our daily habits as the Elizabethan period. But that is a special modern situation. The anthropologists and folk-lorists do not imagine any conditions of that kind. But if they are dealing with unlettered oral transmission, then they should all the more reflect that in that case they are dealing with items whose primary object was story-building, and whose primary reason for survival was the same. The Frog King (see p. 66) is not a *Credo*, nor a manual of totem-law: it is a queer tale with a plain moral.

C (p. 39)

As far as my knowledge goes, children who have an early bent for writing have no special inclination to attempt the writing of fairy-stories, unless that has been almost the sole form of literature presented to them; and they fail most markedly when they try. It is not an easy form. If children have any special leaning it is to Beast-fable, which adults often confuse with Fairy-story. The best stories by children that I have seen have been either 'realistic' (in intent), or have had as their characters animals and birds, who were in the main the zoomorphic human beings usual in Beast-fable. I imagine that this form is so often adopted principally because it allows a large measure of realism: the representation of domestic events and talk that children really know. The form itself is, however, as a rule, suggested or imposed by adults. It has a curious preponderance in the literature, good and bad, that is nowadays commonly presented to young children: I suppose it is felt to go with 'Natural History', semi-scientific books about beasts and birds that are also considered to be proper pabulum for the young. And it is reinforced by the bears and rabbits that seem in recent times almost to have ousted human dolls from the play-rooms even of little girls. Children make up sagas, often long and elaborate, about their dolls. If these are shaped like bears, bears will be the characters of the sagas; but they will talk like people.

D (p. 44)

I was introduced to zoology and palaeontology ('for children') quite as early as to Faërie. I saw pictures of living beasts and of true (so I was told) prehistoric animals. I liked the 'prehistoric' animals best: they had at least lived long ago, and hypothesis (based on somewhat slender evidence) cannot avoid a gleam of fantasy. But I did not like being told that these creatures were 'dragons'. I can still re-feel the irritation that I felt in childhood at assertions of instructive relatives (or their gift-books) such as these: 'snowflakes are fairy jewels', or 'are more beautiful than fairy jewels'; 'the marvels of the ocean depths are more wonderful than fairyland'. Children expect the differences they feel but cannot analyse to be explained by their elders, or at least recognised, not to be ignored or denied. I was keenly alive to the beauty of 'Real things', but it seemed to me quibbling to confuse this with the wonder of 'Other things'. I was eager to study Nature, actually more eager than I was to read most fairy-stories; but I did not want to be quibbled into Science and cheated out of Faërie by people who seemed to assume that by some kind of original sin I should prefer fairy-tales, but according to some kind of new religion I ought to be induced to like science. Nature is no doubt a life-study, or a study for eternity (for those so gifted); but there is a part of man which is not 'Nature', and which therefore is not obliged to study it, and is, in fact, wholly unsatisfied by it.

E (p. 51)

There is, for example, in surrealism commonly present a morbidity or un-ease very rarely found in literary fantasy. The mind that produced the depicted images may often be suspected to have been in fact already morbid; yet this is not a necessary explanation in all cases. A curious disturbance of the mind is often set up by the very act of drawing things of this kind, a state similar in quality and consciousness of morbidity to the sensations in a high fever, when the mind develops a distressing fecundity and facility in figure-making, seeing forms sinister or grotesque in all visible objects about it.

I am speaking here, of course, of the primary expression of Fantasy in 'pictorial' arts, not of 'illustrations'; nor of the cinematograph. However good in themselves, illustrations do little good to fairy-stories. The radical distinction between all art (including drama) that offers a *visible* presentation and true literature is that it imposes one visible form. Literature works from mind to mind and is thus more progenitive. It is at once more universal and more poignantly particular. If it speaks of *bread* or *wine* or *stone* or *tree*, it appeals to the whole of these things, to their ideas; yet each hearer will give to them a peculiar personal embodiment in his imagination. Should the story say 'he ate bread', the dramatic producer or painter can only show 'a piece of bread' according to his taste or fancy, but the hearer of the story will think of bread in general and picture it in some form of his own. If a story says 'he climbed a hill and saw a river in the valley below', the illustrator may catch, or nearly catch, his own vision of such a scene; but every hearer of the words will have his own picture, and it will be made out of all the hills and rivers and dales he has ever seen, but specially out of The Hill, The River, The Valley which were for him the first embodiment of the word.

F (p. 53)

I am referring, of course, primarily to fantasy of forms and visible shapes. Drama can be made out of the impact upon human characters of some event of Fantasy, or Faërie, that requires no machinery, or that can be assumed or reported to have happened. But that is not fantasy in dramatic result; the human characters hold the stage and upon them attention is concentrated. Drama of this sort (exemplified by some of Barrie's plays) can be used frivolously, or it can be used for satire, or for conveying such 'messages' as the playwright may have in his mind – for men. Drama is anthropocentric. Fairy-story and Fantasy need not be. There are, for instance, many stories telling how men and women have disappeared and spent years among the fairies, without noticing the passage of time, or appearing to grow older. In *Mary Rose* Barrie wrote a play on this theme. No fairy is seen. The cruelly tormented human beings are there all the time. In spite of the sentimental star and the angelic voices at the end (in the printed version) it is a painful play, and can easily be made diabolic: by substituting (as I have seen it done) the elvish call for 'angel voices' at the end. The non-dramatic fairy-stories, in so far as they are concerned with the human victims, can also be pathetic or horrible. But they need not be. In most of them the fairies are also there, on equal terms. In some stories they are the real interest. Many of the short folk-lore accounts of such incidents purport to be just pieces of 'evidence' about fairies, items in an agelong accumulation of 'lore' concerning them and the modes of their existence. The sufferings of human beings who come into contact with them (often enough, wilfully) are thus seen in quite a different perspective. A drama could be made about the sufferings of a victim of research in radiology, but hardly about radium itself. But it is possible to be primarily interested in radium (not radiologists) – or primarily interested in Faërie, not tortured mortals. One interest will produce a scientific book, the other a fairy-story. Drama cannot well cope with either.

G (p. 66)

The absence of this sense is a mere hypothesis concerning men of
the lost past, whatever wild confusions men of today, degraded or
deluded, may suffer. It is just as legitimate an hypothesis, and one
more in agreement with what little is recorded concerning the
thoughts of men of old on this subject, that this sense was once
stronger. That fantasies which blended the human form with
animal and vegetable forms, or gave human faculties to beasts, are
ancient is, of course, no evidence for confusion at all. It is, if anything, evidence to the contrary. Fantasy does not blur the sharp
outlines of the real world; for it depends on them. As far as our
western, European, world is concerned, this 'sense of separation'
has in fact been attacked and weakened in modern times not by
fantasy but by scientific theory. Not by stories of centaurs or were-
wolves or enchanted bears, but by the hypotheses (or dogmatic
guesses) of scientific writers who classed Man not only as 'an
animal' – that correct classification is ancient – but as 'only
an animal'. There has been a consequent distortion of sentiment.
The natural love of men not wholly corrupt for beasts, and the
human desire to 'get inside the skin' of living things, has run riot.
We now get men who love animals more than men; who pity
sheep so much that they curse shepherds as wolves; who weep
over a slain warhorse and vilify dead soldiers. It is now, not in the
days when fairy-stories were begotten, that we get 'an absence of
the sense of separation'.

H (p. 68)

The verbal ending – usually held to be as typical of the end of
fairy-stories as 'once upon a time' is of the beginning – 'and they
lived happily ever after' is an artificial device. It does not deceive
anybody. End-phrases of this kind are to be compared to the
margins and frames of pictures, and are no more to be thought
of as the real end of any particular fragment of the seamless Web
of Story than the frame is of the visionary scene, or the casement
of the Outer World. These phrases may be plain or elaborate,
simple or extravagant, as artificial and as necessary as frames

plain, or carved, or gilded. 'And if they have not gone away they are there still.' 'My story is done – see there is a little mouse; anyone who catches it may make himself a fine fur cap of it.' 'And they lived happily ever after.' 'And when the wedding was over, they sent me home with little paper shoes on a causeway of pieces of glass.'

Endings of this sort suit fairy-stories, because such tales have a greater sense and grasp of the endlessness of the World of Story than most modern 'realistic' stories, already hemmed within the narrow confines of their own small time. A sharp cut in the endless tapestry is not unfittingly marked by a formula, even a grotesque or comic one. It was an irresistible development of modern illustration (so largely photographic) that borders should be abandoned and the 'picture' end only with the paper. This method may be suitable for photographs; but it is altogether inappropriate for the pictures that illustrate or are inspired by fairy-stories. An enchanted forest requires a margin, even an elaborate border. To print it conterminous with the page, like a 'shot' of the Rockies in *Picture Post*, as if it were indeed a 'snap' of fairyland or a 'sketch by our artist on the spot', is a folly and an abuse.

As for the beginnings of fairy-stories: one can scarcely improve on the formula *Once upon a time*. It has an immediate effect. This effect can be appreciated by reading, for instance, the fairy-story *The Terrible Head* in the *Blue Fairy Book*. It is Andrew Lang's own adaptation of the story of Perseus and the Gorgon. It begins 'once upon a time', and it does not name any year or land or person. Now this treatment does something which could be called 'turning mythology into fairy-story'. I should prefer to say that it turns high fairy-story (for such is the Greek tale) into a particular form that is at present familiar in our land: a nursery or 'old wives' form. Namelessness is not a virtue but an accident, and should not have been imitated; for vagueness in this regard is a debasement, a corruption due to forgetfulness and lack of skill. But not so, I think, the timelessness. That beginning is not poverty-stricken but significant. It produces at a stroke the sense of a great uncharted world of time.

Leaf by Niggle

THERE was once a little man called Niggle, who had a long journey to make. He did not want to go, indeed the whole idea was distasteful to him; but he could not get out of it. He knew he would have to start some time, but he did not hurry with his preparations.

Niggle was a painter. Not a very successful one, partly because he had many other things to do. Most of these things he thought were a nuisance; but he did them fairly well, when he could not get out of them: which (in his opinion) was far too often. The laws in his country were rather strict. There were other hindrances, too. For one thing, he was sometimes just idle, and did nothing at all. For another, he was kindhearted, in a way. You know the sort of kind heart: it made him uncomfortable more often than it made him do anything; and even when he did anything, it did not prevent him from grumbling, losing his temper, and swearing (mostly to himself). All the same, it did land him in a good many odd jobs for his neighbour, Mr Parish, a man with a lame leg. Occasionally he even helped other people from further off, if they came and asked him to. Also, now and again, he remembered his journey, and began to pack a few things in an ineffectual way: at such times he did not paint very much.

He had a number of pictures on hand; most of them were

too large and ambitious for his skill. He was the sort of painter who can paint leaves better than trees. He used to spend a long time on a single leaf, trying to catch its shape, and its sheen, and the glistening of dewdrops on its edges. Yet he wanted to paint a whole tree, with all of its leaves in the same style, and all of them different.

There was one picture in particular which bothered him. It had begun with a leaf caught in the wind, and it became a tree; and the tree grew, sending out innumerable branches, and thrusting out the most fantastic roots. Strange birds came and settled on the twigs and had to be attended to. Then all round the Tree, and behind it, through the gaps in the leaves and boughs, a country began to open out; and there were glimpses of a forest marching over the land, and of mountains tipped with snow. Niggle lost interest in his other pictures; or else he took them and tacked them on to the edges of his great picture. Soon the canvas became so large that he had to get a ladder; and he ran up and down it, putting in a touch here, and rubbing out a patch there. When people came to call, he seemed polite enough, though he fiddled a little with the pencils on his desk. He listened to what they said, but underneath he was thinking all the time about his big canvas, in the tall shed that had been built for it out in his garden (on a plot where once he had grown potatoes).

He could not get rid of his kind heart. 'I wish I was more strong-minded' he sometimes said to himself, meaning that he wished other people's troubles did not make him feel uncomfortable. But for a long time he was not seriously perturbed. 'At any rate, I shall get this one picture done, my real picture, before I have to go on that wretched journey,' he used to say. Yet he was beginning to see that he could not put off his start indefinitely. The picture would have to stop just growing and get finished.

One day, Niggle stood a little way off from his picture and considered it with unusual attention and detachment. He could not make up his mind what he thought about it, and wished he had some friend who would tell him what to think. Actually it seemed to him wholly unsatisfactory, and yet very lovely, the only really beautiful picture in the world. What he would have liked at that moment would have been to see himself walk in, and slap him on the back and say (with obvious sincerity): 'Absolutely magnificent! I see exactly what you are getting at. Do get on with it, and don't bother about anything else! We will arrange for a public pension, so that you need not.'

However, there was no public pension. And one thing he could see: it would need some concentration, some *work*, hard uninterrupted work, to finish the picture, even at its present size. He rolled up his sleeves, and began to concentrate. He tried for several days not to bother about other things. But there came a tremendous crop of interruptions. Things went wrong in his house; he had to go and serve on a jury in the town; a distant friend fell ill; Mr Parish was laid up with lumbago; and visitors kept on coming. It was springtime, and they wanted a free tea in the country: Niggle lived in a pleasant little house, miles away from the town. He cursed them in his heart, but he could not deny that he had invited them himself, away back in the winter, when he had not thought it an 'interruption' to visit the shops and have tea with acquaintances in the town. He tried to harden his heart; but it was not a success. There were many things that he had not the face to say *no* to, whether he thought them duties or not; and there were some things he was compelled to do, whatever he thought. Some of his visitors hinted that his garden was rather neglected, and that he might get a visit from an Inspector. Very few of them knew about his picture, of course; but if they had known, it would not have made much difference. I doubt if they would have thought that it mattered much. I dare say it was not really a very good picture, though it may have had some good passages. The Tree, at any rate, was curious. Quite unique in its way. So was Niggle; though he was also a very ordinary and rather silly little man.

At length Niggle's time became really precious. His acquaintances in the distant town began to remember that the little man had got to make a troublesome journey, and some began to calculate how long at the latest he could put off starting. They wondered who would take his house, and if the garden would be better kept.

The autumn came, very wet and windy. The little painter was in his shed. He was up on the ladder, trying to catch the gleam of the westering sun on the peak of a snow-mountain, which he had glimpsed just to the left of the leafy tip of one of the Tree's branches. He knew that he would have to be leaving soon: perhaps early next year. He could only just get the picture finished, and only so so, at that: there were some corners where he would not have time now to do more than hint at what he wanted.

There was a knock on the door. 'Come in!' he said sharply, and climbed down the ladder. He stood on the floor twiddling his brush. It was his neighbour, Parish: his only real neighbour, all other folk lived a long way off. Still, he did not like the man very much: partly because he was so often in trouble and in need of help; and also because he did not care about painting, but was very critical about gardening. When Parish looked at Niggle's garden (which was often) he saw mostly weeds; and when he looked at Niggle's pictures (which was seldom) he saw only green and grey patches and black lines, which seemed to him nonsensical. He did not mind mentioning the weeds (a neighbourly duty), but he refrained from giving any opinion of the pictures. He thought this was very kind, and he did not realise that, even if it was kind, it was not kind enough. Help with the weeds (and perhaps praise for the pictures) would have been better.

'Well, Parish, what is it?' said Niggle.

'I oughtn't to interrupt you, I know,' said Parish (without a glance at the picture). 'You are very busy, I'm sure.'

Niggle had meant to say something like that himself, but he had missed his chance. All he said was: 'Yes.'

'But I have no one else to turn to,' said Parish.

'Quite so,' said Niggle with a sigh: one of those sighs that are a private comment, but which are not made quite inaudible. 'What can I do for you?'

'My wife has been ill for some days, and I am getting worried,' said Parish. 'And the wind has blown half the tiles off my roof, and water is pouring into the bedroom. I think I ought to get the doctor. And the builders, too, only they take so long to come. I was wondering if you had any wood and canvas you could spare, just to patch me up and see me through for a day or two.' Now he did look at the picture.

'Dear, dear!' said Niggle. 'You *are* unlucky. I hope it is no more than a cold that your wife has got. I'll come round presently, and help you move the patient downstairs.'

'Thank you very much,' said Parish, rather coolly. 'But it is not a cold, it is a fever. I should not have bothered you for a cold. And my wife is in bed downstairs already. I can't get up and down with trays, not with my leg. But I see you are busy. Sorry to have troubled you. I had rather hoped you might have been able to spare the time to go for the doctor, seeing how I'm placed; and the builder too, if you really have no canvas you can spare.'

'Of course,' said Niggle; though other words were in his

heart, which at the moment was merely soft without feeling at all kind. 'I could go. I'll go, if you are really worried.'

'I am worried, very worried. I wish I was not lame,' said Parish.

So Niggle went. You see, it was awkward. Parish was his neighbour, and everyone else a long way off. Niggle had a bicycle, and Parish had not, and could not ride one. Parish had a lame leg, a genuine lame leg which gave him a good deal of pain: that had to be remembered, as well as his sour expression and whining voice. Of course, Niggle had a picture and barely time to finish it. But it seemed that this was a thing that Parish had to reckon with and not Niggle. Parish, however, did not reckon with pictures; and Niggle could not alter that. 'Curse it!' he said to himself, as he got out his bicycle.

It was wet and windy, and daylight was waning. 'No more work for me today!' thought Niggle, and all the time that he was riding, he was either swearing to himself, or imagining the strokes of his brush on the mountain, and on the spray of leaves beside it, that he had first imagined in the spring. His fingers twitched on the handlebars. Now he was out of the shed, he saw exactly the way in which to treat that shining spray which framed the distant vision of the mountain. But he had a sinking feeling in his heart, a sort of fear that he would never now get a chance to try it out.

Niggle found the doctor, and he left a note at the builder's. The office was shut, and the builder had gone home to his fireside. Niggle got soaked to the skin, and caught a chill himself. The doctor did not set out as promptly as Niggle had done. He arrived next day, which was quite convenient for him, as by that time there were two patients to deal with, in neighbouring houses. Niggle was in bed, with a high temperature, and marvellous patterns of leaves and involved branches forming in his head and on the ceiling. It did not comfort him to learn that Mrs Parish had only had a cold, and was getting up. He turned his face to the wall and buried himself in leaves.

He remained in bed some time. The wind went on blowing. It took away a good many more of Parish's tiles, and some of Niggle's as well: his own roof began to leak. The builder did not come. Niggle did not care; not for a day or two. Then he crawled out to look for some food (Niggle had no wife). Parish did not come round: the rain had got into his leg and made it ache; and his wife was busy mopping up water, and wondering if 'that Mr Niggle' had forgotten to call at the builder's. Had she seen any chance of borrowing anything useful, she would have sent Parish round, leg or no leg; but she did not, so Niggle was left to himself.

At the end of a week or so Niggle tottered out to his shed again. He tried to climb the ladder, but it made his head giddy. He sat and looked at the picture, but there were no patterns of leaves or visions of mountains in his mind that day. He could have painted a far-off view of a sandy desert, but he had not the energy.

Next day he felt a good deal better. He climbed the ladder, and began to paint. He had just begun to get into it again, when there came a knock on the door.

'Damn!' said Niggle. But he might just as well have said 'Come in!' politely, for the door opened all the same. This time a very tall man came in, a total stranger.

'This is a private studio,' said Niggle. 'I am busy. Go away!'

'I am an Inspector of Houses,' said the man, holding up his appointment-card, so that Niggle on his ladder could see it.

'Oh!' he said.

'Your neighbour's house is not satisfactory at all,' said the Inspector.

'I know,' said Niggle. 'I took a note to the builders a long time ago, but they have never come. Then I have been ill.'

'I see,' said the Inspector. 'But you are not ill now.'

'But I'm not a builder. Parish ought to make a complaint to the Town Council, and get help from the Emergency Service.'

'They are busy with worse damage than any up here,' said the Inspector. 'There has been a flood in the valley, and many families are homeless. You should have helped your neighbour to make temporary repairs and prevent the damage from getting more costly to mend than necessary. That is the law. There is plenty of material here: canvas, wood, waterproof paint.'

'Where?' asked Niggle indignantly.

'There!' said the Inspector, pointing to the picture.

'My picture!' exclaimed Niggle.

'I dare say it is,' said the Inspector. 'But houses come first. That is the law.'

'But I can't . . .' Niggle said no more, for at that moment another man came in. Very much like the Inspector he was, almost his double: tall, dressed all in black.

'Come along!' he said. 'I am the Driver.'

Niggle stumbled down from the ladder. His fever seemed to have come on again, and his head was swimming; he felt cold all over.

'Driver? Driver?' he chattered. 'Driver of what?'

'You, and your carriage,' said the man. 'The carriage was ordered long ago. It has come at last. It's waiting. You start today on your journey, you know.'

'There now!' said the Inspector. 'You'll have to go; but it's a bad way to start on your journey, leaving your jobs undone. Still, we can at least make some use of this canvas now.'

'Oh, dear!' said poor Niggle, beginning to weep. 'And it's not even finished!'

'Not finished!' said the Driver. 'Well, it's finished with, as far as you're concerned, at any rate. Come along!'

Niggle went, quite quietly. The Driver gave him no time to pack, saying that he ought to have done that before, and they would miss the train; so all Niggle could do was to grab a little bag in the hall. He found that it contained only a paint-box and a small book of his own sketches: neither food nor clothes. They caught the train all right. Niggle was feeling very tired and sleepy; he was hardly aware of what was going on when they bundled him into his compartment. He did not care much: he had forgotten where he was supposed to be going, or what he was going for. The train ran almost at once into a dark tunnel.

Niggle woke up in a very large, dim railway station. A Porter went along the platform shouting, but he was not shouting the name of the place; he was shouting *Niggle!*

Niggle got out in a hurry, and found that he had left his little bag behind. He turned back, but the train had gone away.

'Ah, there you are!' said the Porter. 'This way! What! No luggage? You will have to go to the Workhouse.'

Niggle felt very ill, and fainted on the platform. They put him in an ambulance and took him to the Workhouse Infirmary.

He did not like the treatment at all. The medicine they gave him was bitter. The officials and attendants were un-friendly, silent, and strict; and he never saw anyone else, except a very severe doctor, who visited him occasionally. It was more like being in a prison than in a hospital. He had to work hard, at stated hours: at digging, carpentry, and paint-ing bare boards all one plain colour. He was never allowed outside, and the windows all looked inwards. They kept him in the dark for hours at a stretch, 'to do some thinking,' they said. He lost count of time. He did not even begin to feel better, not if that could be judged by whether he felt any pleasure in doing anything. He did not, not even in getting into bed.

At first, during the first century or so (I am merely giving his impressions), he used to worry aimlessly about the past. One thing he kept on repeating to himself, as he lay in the dark: 'I wish I had called on Parish the first morning after the high winds began. I meant to. The first loose tiles would have been easy to fix. Then Mrs Parish might never have caught cold. Then I should not have caught cold either. Then I should have had a week longer.' But in time he forgot what it was that he had wanted a week longer for. If he worried at all after that, it was about his jobs in the hospital. He planned them out, thinking how quickly he could stop that board creaking, or rehang that door, or mend that table-leg. Probably he really became rather useful, though no one ever told him so. But that, of course, cannot have been the reason why they kept the poor little man so long. They may have been waiting for him to get better, and judging 'better' by some odd medical standard of their own.

At any rate, poor Niggle got no pleasure out of life, not what he had been used to call pleasure. He was certainly not amused. But it could not be denied that he began to have a feeling of – well satisfaction: bread rather than jam. He could take up a task the moment one bell rang, and lay it aside promptly the moment the next one went, all tidy and ready to be continued at the right time. He got through quite a lot in a day, now; he finished small things off neatly. He had no 'time of his own' (except alone in his bed-cell), and yet he was becoming master of his time; he began to know just what he could do with it. There was no sense of rush. He was quieter inside now, and at resting-time he could really rest.

Then suddenly they changed all his hours; they hardly let him go to bed at all; they took him off carpentry altogether and kept him at plain digging, day after day. He took it fairly well. It was a long while before he even began to grope in the back of his mind for the curses that he had practically forgotten. He went on digging, till his back seemed broken, his hands were raw, and he felt that he could not manage another spadeful. Nobody thanked him. But the doctor came and looked at him.

'Knock off!' he said. 'Complete rest – in the dark.'

Niggle was lying in the dark, resting completely; so that, as he had not been either feeling or thinking at all, he might have been lying there for hours or for years, as far as he could tell. But now he heard Voices: not voices that he had ever heard before. There seemed to be a Medical Board, or perhaps a Court of Inquiry, going on close at hand, in an adjoining room with the door open, possibly, though he could not see any light.

'Now the Niggle case,' said a Voice, a severe voice, more severe than the doctor's.

'What was the matter with him?' said a Second Voice, a voice that you might have called gentle, though it was not soft – it was a voice of authority, and sounded at once hopeful and sad. 'What was the matter with Niggle? His heart was in the right place.'

'Yes, but it did not function properly,' said the First Voice. 'And his head was not screwed on tight enough: he hardly ever thought at all. Look at the time he wasted, not even amusing himself! He never got ready for his journey. He was moderately well-off, and yet he arrived here almost destitute, and had to be put in the paupers' wing. A bad case, I am afraid. I think he should stay some time yet.'

'It would not do him any harm, perhaps,' said the Second Voice. 'But, of course, he is only a little man. He was never meant to be anything very much; and he was never very strong. Let us look at the Records. Yes. There are some favourable points, you know.'

'Perhaps,' said the First Voice; 'but very few that will really bear examination.'

'Well,' said the Second Voice, 'there are these. He was a painter by nature. In a minor way, of course; still, a Leaf by Niggle has a charm of its own. He took a great deal of pains with leaves, just for their own sake. But he never thought that that made him important. There is no note in the Records of his pretending, even to himself, that it excused his neglect of things ordered by the law.'

'Then he should not have neglected so many,' said the First Voice.

'All the same, he did answer a good many Calls.'

'A small percentage, mostly of the easier sort, and he called those Interruptions. The Records are full of the word, together with a lot of complaints and silly imprecations.'

'True; but they looked like interruptions to him, of course, poor little man. And there is this: he never expected any Return, as so many of his sort call it. There is the Parish case, the one that came in later. He was Niggle's neighbour, never did a stroke for him, and seldom showed any gratitude at all. But there is no note in the Records that Niggle expected Parish's gratitude; he does not seem to have thought about it.'

'Yes, that is a point,' said the First Voice; 'but rather small. I think you will find Niggle often merely forgot. Things he had to do for Parish he put out of his mind as a nuisance he had done with.'

'Still, there is this last report,' said the Second Voice, 'that wet bicycle-ride. I rather lay stress on that. It seems plain that this was a genuine sacrifice: Niggle guessed that he was throwing away his last chance with his picture, and he guessed, too, that Parish was worrying unnecessarily.'

'I think you put it too strongly,' said the First Voice. 'But you have the last word. It is your task, of course, to put the best interpretation on the facts. Sometimes they will bear it. What do you propose?'

'I think it is a case for a little gentle treatment now,' said the Second Voice.

Niggle thought that he had never heard anything so generous as that Voice. It made Gentle Treatment sound like a load of rich gifts, and the summons to a King's feast. Then suddenly Niggle felt ashamed. To hear that he was considered a case for Gentle Treatment overwhelmed him, and made him blush in the dark. It was like being publicly praised, when you and all the audience knew that the praise was not deserved. Niggle hid his blushes in the rough blanket.

There was a silence. Then the First Voice spoke to Niggle, quite close. 'You have been listening,' it said.

'Yes,' said Niggle.

'Well, what have you to say?'

'Could you tell me about Parish?' said Niggle. 'I should like to see him again. I hope he is not very ill? Can you cure his leg? It used to give him a wretched time. And please don't worry about him and me. He was a very good neighbour, and let me have excellent potatoes, very cheap which saved me a lot of time.'

'Did he?' said the First Voice. 'I am glad to hear it.'

There was another silence. Niggle heard the Voices receding. 'Well, I agree,' he heard the First Voice say in the distance. 'Let him go on to the next stage. Tomorrow, if you like.'

Niggle woke up to find that his blinds were drawn, and his little cell was full of sunshine. He got up, and found that some comfortable clothes had been put out for him, not hospital uniform. After breakfast the doctor treated his sore hands, putting some salve on them that healed them at once. He gave Niggle some good advice, and a bottle of tonic (in case he needed it). In the middle of the morning they gave Niggle a biscuit and a glass of wine; and then they gave him a ticket.

'You can go to the railway station now,' said the doctor. 'The Porter will look after you. Good-bye.'

Niggle slipped out of the main door, and blinked a little. The sun was very bright. Also he had expected to walk out into a large town, to match the size of the station; but he did not. He was on the top of a hill, green, bare, swept by a keen invigorating wind. Nobody else was about. Away down under the hill he could see the roof of the station shining.

He walked downhill to the station briskly, but without hurry. The Porter spotted him at once.

'This way!' he said, and led Niggle to a bay, in which there was a very pleasant little local train standing: one coach, and a small engine, both very bright, clean, and newly painted. It looked as if this was their first run. Even the track that lay in front of the engine looked new: the rails shone, the chairs were painted green, and the sleepers gave off a delicious smell of fresh tar in the warm sunshine. The coach was empty.

'Where does this train go, Porter?' asked Niggle.

'I don't think they have fixed its name yet,' said the Porter. 'But you'll find it all right.' He shut the door.

The train moved off at once. Niggle lay back in his seat. The little engine puffed along in a deep cutting with high green banks, roofed with blue sky. It did not seem very long before the engine gave a whistle, the brakes were put on, and the train stopped. There was no station, and no signboard, only a flight of steps up the green embankment. At the top of the steps there was a wicket-gate in a trim hedge. By the gate stood his bicycle; at least, it looked like his, and there was a yellow label tied to the bars with NIGGLE written on it in large black letters.

Niggle pushed open the gate, jumped on the bicycle, and went bowling downhill in the spring sunshine. Before long he found that the path on which he had started had disappeared, and the bicycle was rolling along over a marvellous turf. It was green and close; and yet he could see every blade distinctly. He seemed to remember having seen or dreamed of that sweep of grass somewhere or other. The curves of the land were familiar somehow. Yes: the ground was becoming level, as it should, and now, of course, it was beginning to rise again. A great green shadow came between him and the sun. Niggle looked up, and fell off his bicycle.

Before him stood the Tree, his Tree, finished. If you could say that of a Tree that was alive, its leaves opening, its branches growing and bending in the wind that Niggle had so often felt or guessed, and had so often failed to catch. He gazed at the Tree, and slowly he lifted his arms and opened them wide.

'It's a gift!' he said. He was referring to his art, and also to the result; but he was using the word quite literally.

He went on looking at the Tree. All the leaves he had ever

laboured at were there, as he had imagined them rather than as he had made them; and there were others that had only budded in his mind, and many that might have budded, if only he had had time. Nothing was written on them, they were just exquisite leaves, yet they were dated as clear as a calendar. Some of the most beautiful – and the most characteristic, the most perfect examples of the Niggle style – were seen to have been produced in collaboration with Mr Parish: there was no other way of putting it.

The birds were building in the Tree. Astonishing birds: how they sang! They were mating, hatching, growing wings, and flying away singing into the Forest, even while he looked at them. For now he saw that the Forest was there too, opening out on either side, and marching away into the distance. The Mountains were glimmering far away.

After a time Niggle turned towards the Forest. Not because he was tired of the Tree, but he seemed to have got it all clear in his mind now, and was aware of it, and of its growth, even when he was not looking at it. As he walked away, he discovered an odd thing: the Forest, of course, was a distant Forest, yet he could approach it, even enter it, without its losing that particular charm. He had never before been able to walk into the distance without turning it into mere surroundings. It really added a considerable attraction to walking in the country, because, as you walked, new distances opened out; so that you now had double, treble, and quadruple distances, doubly, trebly, and quadruply enchanting. You could go on and on, and have a whole country in a garden, or in a picture (if you preferred to call it that). You could go on and on, but not perhaps for ever. There were the Mountains in the background. They did get nearer, very slowly. They did not seem to belong to the picture, or only as a link to something else, a glimpse through the trees of something different, a further stage: another picture.

Niggle walked about, but he was not merely pottering. He was looking round carefully. The Tree was finished, though not finished with – 'Just the other way about to what it used to be,' he thought – but in the Forest there were a number of inconclusive regions, that still needed work and thought. Nothing needed altering any longer, nothing was wrong, as far as it had gone, but it needed continuing up to a definite point. Niggle saw the point precisely, in each case.

He sat down under a very beautiful distant tree – a variation of the Great Tree, but quite individual, or it would be with a little more attention – and he considered where to begin work, and where to end it, and how much time was required. He could not quite work out his scheme.

'Of course!' he said. 'What I need is Parish. There are lots of things about earth, plants, and trees that he knows and I don't. This place cannot be left just as my private park. I need help and advice: I ought to have got it sooner.'

He got up and walked to the place where he had decided to begin work. He took off his coat. Then, down in a little sheltered hollow hidden from a further view, he saw a man looking round rather bewildered. He was leaning on a spade, but plainly did not know what to do. Niggle hailed him. 'Parish!' he called.

Parish shouldered his spade and came up to him. He still limped a little. They did not speak, just nodded as they used to do, passing in the lane, but now they walked about together, arm in arm. Without talking, Niggle and Parish agreed exactly where to make the small house and garden, which seemed to be required.

As they worked together, it became plain that Niggle was now the better of the two at ordering his time and getting things done. Oddly enough, it was Niggle who became most absorbed in building and gardening, while Parish often wondered about looking at trees, and especially at the Tree.

One day Niggle was busy planting a quickset hedge, and Parish was lying on the grass near by, looking attentively at a beautiful and shapely little yellow flower growing in the green turf. Niggle had put a lot of them among the roots of his Tree long ago. Suddenly Parish looked up: his face was glistening in the sun, and he was smiling.

'This is grand!' he said. 'I oughtn't to be here, really. Thank you for putting in a word for me.'

'Nonsense,' said Niggle. 'I don't remember what I said, but anyway it was not nearly enough.'

'Oh yes, it was,' said Parish. 'It got me out a lot sooner. That Second Voice, you know: he had me sent here; he said you had asked to see me. I owe it to you.'

'No. You owe it to the Second Voice,' said Niggle. 'We both do.'

They went on living and working together: I do not know how long. It is no use denying that at first they occasionally disagreed, especially when they got tired. For at first they did sometimes get tired. They found that they had both been provided with tonics. Each bottle had the same label: *A few drops to be taken in water from the Spring, before resting.*

They found the Spring in the heart of the Forest; only once long ago had Niggle imagined it, but he had never drawn it. Now he perceived that it was the source of the lake that glimmered, far away and the nourishment of all that grew in the country. The few drops made the water astringent, rather bitter, but invigorating; and it cleared the head. After drinking they rested alone; and then they got up again and things went on merrily. At such times Niggle would think of wonderful new flowers and plants, and Parish always knew exactly how to set them and where they would do best. Long before the tonics were finished they had ceased to need them. Parish lost his limp.

As their work drew to an end they allowed themselves more and more time for walking about, looking at the trees, and the flowers, and the lights and shapes, and the lie of the land. Sometimes they sang together; but Niggle found that he was now beginning to turn his eyes, more and more often, towards the Mountains.

The time came when the house in the hollow, the garden, the grass, the forest, the lake, and all the country was nearly complete, in its own proper fashion. The Great Tree was in full blossom.

'We shall finish this evening,' said Parish one day. 'After that we will go for a really long walk.'

They set out next day, and they walked until they came right through the distances to the Edge. It was not visible, of course: there was no line, or fence, or wall; but they knew that they had come to the margin of that country. They saw a man, he looked like a shepherd; he was walking towards them, down the grass-slopes that led up into the Mountains.

'Do you want a guide?' he asked. 'Do you want to go on?'

For a moment a shadow fell between Niggle and Parish, for Niggle knew that he did now want to go on, and (in a sense) ought to go on; but Parish did not want to go on, and was not yet ready to go.

'I must wait for my wife,' said Parish to Niggle. 'She'd be lonely. I rather gathered that they would send her after me, some time or other, when she was ready, and when I had got things ready for her. The house is finished now, as well as we could make it; but I should like to show it to her. She'll be able to make it better, I expect: more homely. I hope she'll like this country, too.' He turned to the shepherd. 'Are you a guide?' he asked. 'Could you tell me the name of this country?'

'Don't you know?' said the man. 'It is Niggle's Country. It is Niggle's Picture, or most of it: a little of it is now Parish's Garden.'

'Niggle's Picture!' said Parish in astonishment. 'Did *you* think of all this, Niggle? I never knew you were so clever. Why didn't you tell me?'

'He tried to tell you long ago,' said the man, 'but you would not look. He had only got canvas and paint in those days, and you wanted to mend your roof with them. This is what you and your wife used to call Niggle's Nonsense, or That Daubing.'

'But it did not look like this then, not *real*,' said Parish.

'No, it was only a glimpse then,' said the man; 'but you might have caught the glimpse, if you had ever thought it worth while to try.'

'I did not give you much chance,' said Niggle. 'I never tried to explain. I used to call you Old Earth-grubber. But what does it matter? We have lived and worked together now. Things might have been different, but they could not have been better. All the same, I am afraid I shall have to be going on. We shall meet again, I expect: there must be many more things we can do together. Goodbye!' He shook Parish's hand warmly: a good, firm, honest hand it seemed. He turned and looked back for a moment. The blossom on the Great Tree was shining like flame. All the birds were flying in the air and singing. Then he smiled and nodded to Parish and went off with the shepherd.

He was going to learn about sheep, and the high pasturages, and look at a wider sky, and walk ever further and further towards the Mountains, always uphill. Beyond that I cannot guess what became of him. Even little Niggle in his old home could glimpse the Mountains far away, and they got into the borders of his picture; but what they are really like, and what lies beyond them only those can say who have climbed them.

'I think he was a silly little man,' said Councillor Tompkins. 'Worthless, in fact; no use to Society at all.'

'Oh, I don't know,' said Atkins, who was nobody of importance, just a schoolmaster. 'I am not so sure: it depends on what you mean by use.'

'No practical or economic use,' said Tompkins. 'I dare say he could have been made into a serviceable cog of some sort, if you schoolmasters knew your business. But you don't, and so we get useless people of his sort. If I ran this country I should put him and his like to some job that they're fit for, washing dishes in a communal kitchen or something, and I should see that they did it properly. Or I would put them away. I should have put *him* away long ago.'

'Put him away? You mean you'd have made him start on the journey before his time?'

'Yes, if you must use that meaningless old expression. Push him through the tunnel into the great Rubbish Heap: that's what I mean.'

'Then you don't think painting is worth anything, not worth preserving, or improving, or even making use of?'

'Of course, painting has uses,' said Tompkins. 'But you couldn't make use of his painting. There is plenty of scope for bold young men not afraid of new ideas and new methods. None for this old-fashioned stuff. Private day-dreaming. He could not have designed a telling poster to save his life. Always fiddling with leaves and flowers. I asked him why, once. He said he thought they were pretty! Can you believe it? He said *pretty*! 'What, digestive and genital organs of plants?' I said to him; and he had nothing to answer. Silly footler.'

'Footler,' sighed Atkins. 'Yes, poor little man, he never finished anything. Ah well, his canvases have been put to "better uses", since he went. But I am not so sure, Tompkins. You remember that large one, the one they used to patch the damaged house next door to his, after the gales and floods? I found a corner of it torn off, lying in a field. It was damaged, but legible: a mountain-peak and a spray of leaves. I can't get it out of my mind.'

'Out of your what?' said Tompkins.

'Who are you two talking about?' said Perkins, intervening in the cause of peace: Atkins had flushed rather red.

'The name's not worth repeating,' said Tompkins. 'I don't know why we are talking about him at all. He did not live in town.'

'No,' said Atkins; 'but you had your eye on his house, all the same. That is why you used to go and call, and sneer at him while drinking his tea. Well, you've got his house now, as well as the one in town, so you need not grudge him his name. We were talking about Niggle, if you want to know, Perkins.'

'Oh, poor little Niggle!' said Perkins. 'Never knew he painted.'

That was probably the last time Niggle's name ever came up in conversation. However, Atkins preserved the odd corner. Most of it crumbled; but one beautiful leaf remained intact. Atkins had it framed. Later he left it to the Town Museum, and for a long time while 'Leaf: by Niggle' hung there in a recess, and was noticed by a few eyes. But eventually the Museum was burnt down, and the leaf, and Niggle, were entirely forgotten in his old country.

'It is proving very useful indeed,' said the Second Voice. 'As a holiday, and a refreshment. It is splendid for con-valescence; and not only for that, for many it is the best introduction to the Mountains. It works wonders in some cases. I am sending more and more there. They seldom have to come back.'

'No, that is so,' said the First Voice. 'I think we shall have to give the region a name. What do you propose?'

'The Porter settled that some time ago,' said the Second Voice. '*Train for Niggle's Parish in the bay*: he has shouted that for a long while now. Niggle's Parish. I sent a message to both of them to tell them.'

'What did they say?'

'They both laughed. Laughed – the Mountains rang with it!'

Smith of
Wootton Major

Smith of
Wootton Major

Illustrations by Pauline Baynes

Smith of
Wootton Major

HERE was a village once, not very long ago for those with long memories, nor very far away for those with long legs. Wootton Major it was called because it was larger than Wootton Minor, a few miles away deep in the trees; but it was not very large, though it was at that time prosperous, and a fair number of folk lived in it, good, bad, and mixed, as is usual.

It was a remarkable village in its way, being well known in the country round about for the skill of its workers in various crafts, but most of all for its cooking. It had a large Kitchen which belonged to the Village Council, and the Master Cook was an important person. The Cook's House and the Kitchen adjoined the Great Hall, the largest and oldest building in the place and the most beautiful. It was built of good stone and good oak and was well tended, though it was no longer painted or gilded as it had been once upon a time. In the Hall the villagers held their meetings and debates, and their public feasts, and their family gatherings. So the Cook was kept busy, since for all these occasions he had to provide suitable fare. For the festivals, of which there were many in the course of a year, the fare that was thought suitable was plentiful and rich.

There was one festival to which all looked forward, for it was the only one held in winter. It went on for a week, and on its last day at sundown there was a merrymaking called The Feast of Good Children, to which not many were invited. No doubt some who deserved to be asked were overlooked, and some who did not were invited by mistake; for that is the way of things, however careful those who arrange such matters may try to be. In any case it was largely by chance of birthday that any child came in for the Twenty-four Feast, since that was only held once in twenty-four years, and only twenty-four children were invited. For that occasion the Master Cook was expected to do his best, and in addition to many other good things it was the custom for him to make the Great Cake. By the excellence (or otherwise) of this his name was chiefly remembered, for a Master Cook seldom if ever lasted long enough in office to make a second Great Cake.

There came a time, however, when the reigning Master Cook, to everyone's surprise, since it had never happened before, suddenly announced that he needed a holiday; and he went away, no one knew where; and when he came back some months later he seemed rather changed. He had been a kind man who liked to see other people enjoying themselves, but he was himself serious, and said very little. Now he was merrier, and often said and did most laughable things; and at feasts he would himself sing gay songs which was not expected of Master Cooks. Also he brought back with him an Apprentice; and that astonished the Village.

It was not astonishing for the Master Cook to have an apprentice. It was usual. The Master chose one in due time, and he taught him all that he could; and as they both grew older the apprentice took on more of the important work, so that when the Master retired or died there he was, ready to take over the office and become Master Cook in his turn. But this Master had never chosen an apprentice. He had always said 'time enough yet', or 'I'm keeping my eyes open and I'll choose one when I find one to suit me.' But now he brought with him a mere boy, and not one from the village. He was more lithe than the Wootton lads and quicker, soft-spoken and very polite, but ridiculously young for the work, barely in his teens by the look of him. Still, choosing his apprentice was the Master Cook's affair, and no one had the right to interfere in it; so the boy remained and stayed in the Cook's House until he was old enough to find lodgings for himself. People soon became used to seeing him about, and he made a few friends. They and the Cook called him Alf, but to the rest he was just Prentice.

The next surprise came only three years later. One spring morning the Master Cook took off his tall white hat, folded up his clean aprons, hung up his white coat, took a stout ash stick and a small bag, and departed. He said goodbye to the apprentice. No one else was about.

'Goodbye for now, Alf,' he said. 'I leave you to manage things as best you can, which is always very well. I expect it will turn out all right. If we meet again, I hope to hear all about it. Tell them that I've gone on another holiday, but this time I shan't be coming back again.'

There was quite a stir in the village when Prentice gave this message to people who came to the Kitchen. 'What a thing to do!' they said. 'And without warning or farewell! What are we going to do without any Master Cook? He has left no one to take his place.' In all their discussions no one ever thought of making young Prentice into Cook. He had grown a bit taller but still looked like a boy, and he had only served for three years.

In the end for lack of anyone better they appointed a man

of the village, who could cook well enough in a small way. When he was younger he had helped the Master at busy times, but the Master had never taken to him and would not have him as apprentice. He was now a solid sort of man with a wife and children, and careful with money. 'At any rate he won't go off without notice,' they said, 'and poor cooking is better than none. It is seven years till the next Great Cake, and by that time he should be able to manage it.'

Nokes, for that was his name, was very pleased with the turn things had taken. He had always wished to become Master Cook, and had never doubted that he could manage it. For some time, when he was alone in the Kitchen, he used to put on the tall white hat and look at himself in a polished frying pan and say: 'How do you do, Master. That hat suits you properly, might have been made for you. I hope things go well with you.'

Things went well enough; for at first Nokes did his best, and he had Prentice to help him. Indeed he learned a lot from him by watching him slyly, though that Nokes never admitted. But in due course the time for the Twenty-four Feast drew near, and Nokes had to think about making the Great Cake. Secretly he was worried about it, for although with seven years' practice he could turn out passable cakes and pastries for ordinary occasions, he knew that his Great Cake would be eagerly awaited, and would have to satisfy severe critics. Not only the children. A smaller cake of the same materials and baking had to be provided for those who came to help at the feast. Also it was expected that the Great Cake should have something novel and surprising about it and not be a mere repetition of the one before.

His chief notion was that it should be very sweet and rich; and he decided that it should be entirely covered in sugar-icing (at which Prentice had a clever hand). 'That will make it pretty and fairylike,' he thought. Fairies and sweets were two of the very few notions he had about the tastes of children. Fairies he thought one grew out of; but of sweets he remained very fond. 'Ah! fairylike,' he said, 'that gives me an idea'; and so it came into his head that he would stick a little doll on a pinnacle in the middle of the Cake, dressed all in white, with a little wand in her hand ending in a tinsel star, and *Fairy Queen* written in pink icing round her feet.

But when he began preparing the materials for the cake-making he found that he had only dim memories of what should go *inside* a Great Cake; so he looked in some old books of recipes left behind by previous cooks. They puzzled him, even when he could make out their handwriting, for they mentioned many things that he had not heard of, and some that he had forgotten and now had no time to get; but he thought he might try one or two of the spices that the books spoke of. He scratched his head and remembered an old black box with several different compartments in which the last Cook had once kept spices and other things for special cakes. He had not looked at it since he took over, but after a search he found it on a high shelf in the store-room.

He took it down and blew the dust off the lid; but when he opened it he found that very little of the spices was left, and they were dry and musty. But in one compartment in the corner he discovered a small star, hardly as big as one of our sixpences, black-looking as if it was made of silver but was tarnished. 'That's funny!' he said as he held it up to the light.

'No, it isn't!' said a voice behind him, so suddenly that he jumped. It was the voice of Prentice, and he had never spoken to the Master in that tone before. Indeed he seldom spoke to Nokes at all unless he was spoken to first. Very right and proper in a youngster; he might be clever with icing but he had a lot to learn yet: that was Nokes's opinion.

'What do you mean, young fellow?' he said, not much pleased. 'If it isn't funny what is it?'

'It is *fay*,' said Prentice. 'It comes from Faery.'

Then the Cook laughed. 'All right, all right,' he said. 'It means much the same; but call it that if you like. You'll grow up some day. Now you can get on with stoning the raisins. If you notice any funny fairy ones, tell me.'

'What are you going to do with the star, Master?' said Prentice.

'Put it into the Cake, of course,' said the Cook. 'Just the thing, especially if it's *fairy*,' he sniggered. 'I daresay you've been to children's parties yourself, and not so long ago either, where little trinkets like this were stirred into the mixture, and little coins and what not. Anyway we do that in this village; it amuses the children.'

'But this isn't a trinket, Master, it's a fay-star,' said Prentice.

'So you've said already,' snapped the Cook. 'Very well, I'll tell the children. It'll make them laugh.'

'I don't think it will, Master,' said Prentice. 'But it's the right thing to do, quite right.'

'Who do you think you're talking to?' said Nokes.

In time the Cake was made and baked and iced, mostly by Prentice. 'As you are so set on fairies, I'll let you make the Fairy Queen,' Nokes said to him.

'Very good, Master,' he answered. 'I'll do it if you are too busy. But it was your idea and not mine.'

'It's my place to have ideas, and not yours,' said Nokes.

At the Feast the Cake stood in the middle of the long table, inside a ring of twenty-four red candles. Its top rose into a small white mountain, up the sides of which grew little trees glittering as if with frost; on its summit stood a tiny white figure on one foot like a snow-maiden dancing, and in her hand was a minute wand of ice sparkling with light.

The children looked at it with wide eyes, and one or two clapped their hands, crying: 'Isn't it pretty and fairylike!' That delighted the Cook, but the apprentice looked displeased. They were both present: the Master to cut up the Cake when the time came, and the apprentice to sharpen the knife and hand it to him.

At last the Cook took the knife and stepped up to the table. 'I should tell you, my dears,' he said, 'that inside this lovely icing there is a cake made of many nice things to eat; but also stirred well in there are many pretty little things, trinkets and little coins and what not, and I'm told that it is lucky to find one in your slice. There are twenty-four in the Cake, so there should be one for each of you, if the Fairy Queen plays fair. But she doesn't always do so: she's a tricky little creature. You ask Mr Prentice.' The apprentice turned away and studied the faces of the children.

'No! I'm forgetting,' said the Cook. 'There's twenty-five this evening. There's also a little silver star, a special magic one, or so Mr Prentice says. So be careful! If you break one of your pretty front teeth on it, the magic star won't mend it. But I expect it's a specially lucky thing to find, all the same.'

It was a good cake, and no one had any fault to find with it, except that it was no bigger than was needed. When it was all cut up there was a large slice for each of the children, but nothing left over: no coming again. The slices soon disappeared, and every now and then a trinket or a coin was discovered. Some found one, and some found two, and several found none; for that is the way luck goes, whether

T—F

there is a doll with a wand on the cake or not. But when the Cake was all eaten, there was no sign of any magic star.

'Bless me!' said the Cook. 'Then it can't have been made of silver after all; it must have melted. Or perhaps Mr Prentice was right and it was really magical, and it's just vanished and gone back to Fairyland. Not a nice trick to play, I don't think.' He looked at Prentice with a smirk, and Prentice looked at him with dark eyes and did not smile at all.

All the same, the silver star was indeed a fay-star: the apprentice was not one to make mistakes about things of that sort. What had happened was that one of the boys at the Feast had swallowed it without ever noticing it, although he had found a silver coin in his slice and had given it to Nell, the little girl next to him: she looked so disappointed at finding nothing lucky in hers. He sometimes wondered what had really become of the star, and did not know that it had remained with him, tucked away in some place where it could not be felt; for that was what it was intended to do. There it waited for a long time, until its day came.

The Feast had been in mid-winter, but it was now June, and the night was hardly dark at all. The boy got up before dawn, for he did not wish to sleep: it was his tenth birthday. He looked out of the window, and the world seemed quiet and expectant. A little breeze, cool and fragrant, stirred the waking trees. Then the dawn came, and far away he heard the dawn-song of the birds beginning, growing as it came towards him, until it rushed over him, filling all the land round the house, and passed on like a wave of music into the West, as the sun rose above the rim of the world.

'It reminds me of Faery,' he heard himself say; 'but in Faery the people sing too.' Then he began to sing, high and clear, in strange words that he seemed to know by heart; and in that moment the star fell out of his mouth and he caught it on his open hand. It was bright silver now, glistening in the sunlight; but it quivered and rose a little, as if it was about to fly away. Without thinking he clapped his hand to his head, and there the star stayed in the middle of his forehead, and he wore it for many years.

Few people in the village noticed it though it was not invisible to attentive eyes; but it became part of his face, and it did not usually shine at all. Some of its light passed into his eyes; and his voice, which had begun to grow beautiful as soon as the star came to him, became ever more beautiful as he grew up. People liked to hear him speak, even if it was no more than a 'good morning'.

He became well known in his country, not only in his own village but in many others round about, for his good workmanship. His father was a smith, and he followed him in his craft and bettered it. Smithson he was called while his father was still alive, and then just Smith. For by that time he was the best smith between Far Easton and the Westwood and he could make all kinds of things of iron in his smithy. Most of them, of course, were plain and useful, meant for daily needs: farm tools, carpenters' tools, kitchen tools and pots and pans, bars and bolts and hinges, pot-hooks, fire-dogs, and horse-shoes, and the like. They were strong and lasting, but they also had a grace about them, being shapely in their kinds, good to handle and to look at.

But some things, when he had time, he made for delight; and they were beautiful, for he could work iron into wonderful forms that looked as light and delicate as a spray of leaves and blossom, but kept the stern strength of iron, or seemed even stronger. Few could pass by one of the gates or lattices that he made without stopping to admire it; no one could pass through it once it was shut. He sang when he was making things of this sort; and when Smith began to sing those nearby stopped their own work and came to the smithy to listen.

That was all that most people knew about him. It was enough indeed and more than most men and women in the village achieved, even those who were skilled and hard-working. But there was more to know. For Smith became acquainted with Faery, and some regions of it he knew as well as any mortal can; though since too many had become like Nokes, he spoke of this to few people, except his wife and his children. His wife was Nell, to whom he gave the silver coin, and his daughter was Nan, and his son was Ned Smithson. From them it could not have been kept secret anyway, for they sometimes saw the star shining on his forehead, when he came back from one of the long walks he would take alone now and then in the evening, or when he returned from a journey.

From time to time he would go off, sometimes walking, sometimes riding, and it was generally supposed that it was on business; and sometimes it was, and sometimes it was not. At any rate not to get orders for work, or to buy pig-iron and charcoal and other supplies, though he attended to such things with care and knew how to turn an honest penny into twopence, as the saying went. But he had business of its own kind in Faery, and he was welcome there; for the star shone bright on his brow, and he was as safe as a mortal can be in that perilous country. The Lesser Evils avoided the star, and from the Greater Evils he was guarded.

For that he was grateful, for he soon became wise and understood that the marvels of Faery cannot be approached without danger, and that many of the Evils cannot be chal-

lenged without weapons of power too great for any mortal to wield. He remained a learner and explorer, not a warrior; and though in time he could have forged weapons that in his own world would have had power enough to become the matter of great tales and be worth a king's ransom, he knew that in Faery they would have been of small account. So among all the things that he made it is not remembered that he ever forged a sword or a spear or an arrow-head.

In Faery at first he walked for the most part quietly among the lesser folk and the gentler creatures in the woods and meads of fair valleys, and by the bright waters in which at night strange stars shone and at dawn the gleaming peaks of far mountains were mirrored. Some of his briefer visits he spent looking only at one tree or one flower; but later in longer journeys he had seen things of both beauty and terror that he could not clearly remember nor report to his friends, though he knew that they dwelt deep in his heart. But some things he did not forget, and they remained in his mind as wonders and mysteries that he often recalled.

When he first began to walk far without a guide he thought he would discover the further bounds of the land; but great mountains rose before him, and going by long ways round about them he came at last to a desolate shore. He stood beside the Sea of Windless Storm where the blue waves like snow-clad hills roll silently out of Unlight to the long strand, bearing the white ships that return from battles on the Dark Marches of which men know nothing. He saw a great ship cast high upon the land, and the waters fell back in foam without a sound. The elven mariners were tall and terrible; their swords shone and their spears glinted and a piercing light was in their eyes. Suddenly they lifted up their voices in a song of triumph, and his heart was shaken with fear,

and he fell upon his face, and they passed over him and went away into the echoing hills.

Afterwards he went no more to that strand, believing that he was in an island realm beleaguered by the Sea, and he turned his mind towards the mountains, desiring to come to the heart of the kingdom. Once in these wanderings he was overtaken by a grey mist and strayed long at a loss, until the mist rolled away and he found that he was in a wide plain. Far off there was a great hill of shadow, and out of that shadow, which was its root, he saw the King's Tree springing up, tower upon tower, into the sky, and its light was like the sun at noon; and it bore at once leaves and flowers and fruits uncounted, and not one was the same as any other that grew on the Tree.

He never saw that Tree again, though he often sought for it. On one such journey climbing into the Outer Mountains he came to a deep dale among them, and at its bottom lay a lake, calm and unruffled though a breeze stirred the woods that surrounded it. In that dale the light was like a red sunset, but the light came up from the lake. From a low cliff that overhung it he looked down, and it seemed that he could see to an immeasurable depth; and there he beheld strange shapes of flame bending and branching and wavering like great weeds in a sea-dingle, and fiery creatures went to and fro among them. Filled with wonder he went down to the water's edge and tried it with his foot, but it was not water: it was harder than stone and sleeker than glass. He stepped on it and he fell heavily, and a ringing boom ran across the lake and echoed in its shores.

At once the breeze rose to a wild Wind, roaring like a great beast, and it swept him up and flung him on the shore, and it drove him up the slopes whirling and falling like a dead leaf. He put his arms about the stem of a young birch and clung to it, and the Wind wrestled fiercely with them, trying to tear him away; but the birch was bent down to the ground by the blast and enclosed him in its branches. When at last the Wind passed on he rose and saw that the birch was naked. It was stripped of every leaf, and it wept, and tears fell from its branches like rain. He set his hand upon its white bark saying: 'Blessed be the birch! What can I do to make amends, or give thanks?' He felt the answer of the tree pass up from his hand: 'Nothing,' it said. 'Go away! The Wind is hunting you. You do not belong here. Go away and never return!'

As he climbed back out of that dale he felt the tears of the birch trickle down his face and they were bitter on his lips. His heart was saddened as he went on his long road, and for some time he did not enter Faery again. But he could not forsake it, and when he returned his desire was still stronger to go deep into the land.

At last he found a road through the Outer Mountains, and he went on till he came to the Inner Mountains, and they were high and sheer and daunting. Yet in the end he found a pass that he could scale, and upon a day of days greatly daring he came through a narrow cleft and looked down, though he did not know it, into the Vale of Evermorn where the green surpasses the green of the meads of Outer Faery as they surpass ours in our springtime. There the air is so lucid that eyes can see the red tongues of birds as they sing on the trees upon the far side of the valley, though that is very wide and the birds are no greater than wrens.

On the inner side the mountains went down in long slopes filled with the sound of bubbling waterfalls, and in great delight he hastened on. As he set foot upon the grass of the

Vale he heard elven voices singing, and on a lawn beside a river bright with lilies he came upon many maidens dancing. The speed and the grace and the ever-changing modes of their movements enchanted him, and he stepped forward towards their ring. Then suddenly they stood still, and a young maiden with flowing hair and kilted skirt came out to meet him.

She laughed as she spoke to him, saying: 'You are becoming bold, Starbrow, are you not? Have you no fear what the Queen might say, if she knew of this? Unless you have her leave.' He was abashed, for he became aware of his own thought and knew that she read it: that the star on his forehead was a passport to go wherever he wished; and now he knew that it was not. But she smiled as she spoke again: 'Come! Now that you are here you shall dance with me'; and she took his hand and led him into the ring.

There they danced together, and for a while he knew what it was to have the swiftness and the power and the joy to accompany her. For a while. But soon as it seemed they halted again, and she stooped and took up a white flower from before her feet, and she set it in his hair. 'Farewell now!' she said. 'Maybe we shall meet again, by the Queen's leave.'

He remembered nothing of the journey home from that meeting, until he found himself riding along the roads in his own country; and in some villages people stared at him in wonder and watched him till he rode out of sight. When he came to his own house his daughter ran out and greeted him with delight – he had returned sooner than was expected, but none too soon for those that awaited him. 'Daddy!' she cried. 'Where have you been? Your star is shining bright!'

When he crossed the threshold the star dimmed again;

but Nell took him by the hand and led him to the hearth, and there she turned and looked at him. 'Dear Man,' she said, 'where have you been and what have you seen? There is a flower in your hair.' She lifted it gently from his head, and it lay on her hand. It seemed like a thing seen from a great distance, yet there it was, and a light came from it that cast shadows on the walls of the room, now growing dark in the evening. The shadow of the man before her loomed up and its great head was bowed over her. 'You look like a giant, Dad,' said his son, who had not spoken before.

The flower did not wither nor grow dim; and they kept it as a secret and a treasure. The smith made a little casket with a key for it, and there it lay and was handed down for many generations in his kin; and those who inherited the key would at times open the casket and look long at the Living Flower, till the casket closed again: the time of its shutting was not theirs to choose.

The years did not halt in the village. Many now had passed. At the Children's Feast when he received the star the smith was not yet ten years old. Then came another Twenty-four Feast, by which time Alf had become Master Cook and had chosen a new apprentice, Harper. Twelve years later the smith had returned with the Living Flower, and now another Children's Twenty-four Feast was due in the winter to come. One day in that year Smith was walking in the woods of Outer Faery, and it was autumn. Golden leaves were on the boughs and red leaves were on the ground. Footsteps came behind him, but he did not heed them or turn round, for he was deep in thought.

On that visit he had received a summons and had made a far journey. Longer it seemed to him than any he had yet made. He was guided and guarded, but he had little memory of the ways that he had taken; for often he had been blind-folded by mist or by shadow, until at last he came to a high place under a night-sky of innumerable stars. There he was brought before the Queen herself. She wore no crown and had no throne. She stood there in her majesty and her glory, and all about her was a great host shimmering and glittering like the stars above; but she was taller than the points of their great spears, and upon her head there burned a white flame. She made a sign for him to approach, and trembling he stepped forward. A high clear trumpet sounded, and be-hold! they were alone.

He stood before her, and he did not kneel in courtesy, for he was dismayed and felt that for one so lowly all gestures were in vain. At length he looked up and beheld her face and her eyes bent gravely upon him; and he was troubled and amazed, for in that moment he knew her again: the fair maid of the Green Vale, the dancer, at whose feet the flowers sprang. She smiled seeing his memory, and drew towards him; and they spoke long together, for the most part without words, and he learned many things in her thought, some of which gave him joy, and others filled him with grief. Then his mind turned back retracing his life until he came to the day of the Children's Feast and the coming of the star, and suddenly he saw again the little dancing figure with its wand, and in shame he lowered his eyes from the Queen's beauty.

But she laughed again as she had laughed in the Vale of Evermorn. 'Do not be grieved for me, Starbrow,' she said. 'Nor too much ashamed of your own folk. Better a little doll, maybe, than no memory of Faery at all. For some the only glimpse. For some the awaking. Ever since that day you have desired in your heart to see me, and I have granted your wish. But I can give you no more. Now at farewell I will make you my messenger. If you meet the King, say to him: *The time has come. Let him choose.*'

'But Lady of Faery,' he stammered, 'where then is the King?' For he had asked this question many times of the people of Faery, and they had all said the same: 'He has not told us.'

And the Queen answered: 'If he has not told you, Starbrow, then I may not. But he makes many journeys and may be met in unlikely places. Now kneel of your courtesy.'

Then he knelt, and she stooped and laid her hand on his head, and a great stillness came upon him; and he seemed to be both in the World and in Faery, and also outside them and surveying them, so that he was at once in bereavement, and in ownership, and in peace. When after a while the stillness passed he raised his head and stood up. The dawn was in the sky and the stars were pale, and the Queen was gone. Far off he heard the echo of a trumpet in the mountains. The high field where he stood was silent and empty; and he knew that his way now led back to bereavement.

That meeting-place was now far behind him, and here he was, walking among the fallen leaves, pondering all that he had seen and learned. The footsteps came nearer. Then suddenly a voice said at his side: 'Are you going my way, Starbrow?'

He started and came out of his thoughts, and he saw a man beside him. He was tall, and he walked lightly and quickly; he was dressed all in dark green and wore a hood that partly overshadowed his face. The smith was puzzled, for only the people of Faery called him 'Starbrow', but he could not remember ever having seen this man there before; and yet he felt uneasily that he should know him. 'What way are you going then?' he said.

'I am going back to your village now,' the man answered, 'and I hope that you are also returning.'

'I am indeed,' said the smith. 'Let us walk together. But now something has come back to my mind. Before I began my homeward journey a Great Lady gave me a message, but we shall soon be passing from Faery, and I do not think that I shall ever return. Will you?'

'Yes, I shall. You may give the message to me.'

'But the message was to the King. Do you know where to find him?'

'I do. What was the message?'

'The Lady only asked me to say to him: *The time has come. Let him choose.*'

'I understand. Trouble yourself no further.'

They went on then side by side in silence save for the rustle of the leaves about their feet; but after a few miles while they were still within the bounds of Faery the man halted. He turned towards the smith and threw back his hood. Then the smith knew him. He was Alf the Prentice, as the smith still called him in his own mind, remembering always the day when as a youth Alf had stood in the Hall, holding the bright knife for the cutting of the Cake, and his eyes had gleamed in the light of the candles. He must be an old man now, for he had been Master Cook for many years; but here standing under the eaves of the Outer Wood he looked like the apprentice of long ago, though more masterly: there was no grey in his hair nor line on his face, and his eyes gleamed as if they reflected a light.

'I should like to speak to you, Smith Smithson, before we go back to your country,' he said. The smith wondered at that, for he himself had often wished to talk to Alf, but had never been able to do so. Alf had always greeted him kindly

and had looked at him with friendly eyes, but had seemed to avoid talking to him alone. He was looking now at the smith with friendly eyes; but he lifted his hand and with his forefinger touched the star on his brow. The gleam left his eyes, and then the smith knew that it had come from the star, and that it must have been shining brightly but now was dimmed. He was surprised and drew away angrily.

'Do you not think, Master Smith,' said Alf, 'that it is time for you to give this thing up?'

'What is that to you, Master Cook?' he answered. 'And why should I do so? Isn't it mine? It came to me, and may a man not keep things that come to him so, at the least as a remembrance?'

'Some things. Those that are free gifts and given for remembrance. But others are not so given. They cannot belong to a man for ever, nor be treasured as heirlooms. They are lent. You have not thought, perhaps, that someone else may need this thing. But it is so. Time is pressing.'

Then the smith was troubled, for he was a generous man, and he remembered with gratitude all that the star had brought to him. 'Then what should I do?' he asked. 'Should I give it to one of the Great in Faery? Should I give it to the King?' And as he said this a hope sprang in his heart that on such an errand he might once more enter Faery.

'You could give it to me,' said Alf, 'but you might find that too hard. Will you come with me to my store-room and put it back in the box where your grandfather laid it?'

'I did not know that,' said the smith.

'No one knew but me. I was the only one with him.'

'Then I suppose that you know how he came by the star, and why he put it in the box?'

'He brought it from Faery: that you know without asking,' Alf answered. 'He left it behind in the hope that it might come to you, his only grandchild. So he told me, for he thought that I could arrange that. He was your mother's father. I do not know whether she told you much about him, if indeed she knew much to tell. Rider was his name, and he was a great traveller: he had seen many things and could do many things before he settled down and became Master Cook. But he went away when you were only two years old – and they could find no one better to follow him than Nokes, poor man. Still, as we expected, I became Master in time. This year I shall make another Great Cake: the only Cook, as far as is remembered, ever to make a second one. I wish to put the star in it.'

'Very well, you shall have it,' said the smith. He looked at Alf as if he was trying to read his thought. 'Do you know who will find it?'

'What is that to you, Master Smith?'

'I should like to know, if you do, Master Cook. It might make it easier for me to part with a thing so dear to me. My daughter's child is too young.'

'It might and it might not. We shall see,' said Alf.

They said no more, and they went on their way until they passed out of Faery and came back at last to the village. Then they walked to the Hall; and in the world the sun was now setting and a red light was in the windows. The gilded carvings on the great door glowed, and strange faces of many colours looked down from the water-spouts under the roof. Not long ago the Hall had been re-glazed and re-painted, and there had been much debate on the Council about it. Some disliked it and called it 'new-fangled', but some with more knowledge knew that it was a return to old custom. Still, since it had cost no one a penny and the Master Cook must have paid for it himself, he was allowed to have his own way. But the smith had not seen it in such a light before, and he stood and looked at the Hall in wonder, forgetting his errand.

He felt a touch on his arm, and Alf led him round to a small door at the back. He opened it and led the smith down a dark passage into the store-room. There he lit a tall candle, and unlocking a cupboard he took down from a shelf the black box. It was polished now and adorned with silver scrolls.

He raised the lid and showed it to the smith. One small compartment was empty; the others were now filled with spices, fresh and pungent, and the smith's eyes began to water. He put his hand to his forehead, and the star came away readily; but he felt a sudden stab of pain, and tears ran down his face. Though the star shone brightly again as it lay in his hand, he could not see it, except as a blurred dazzle of light that seemed far away.

'I cannot see clearly,' he said. 'You must put it in for me.' He held out his hand, and Alf took the star and laid it in its place, and it went dark.

The smith turned away without another word and groped his way to the door. On the threshold he found that his sight had cleared again. It was evening and the Even-star was shining in a luminous sky close to the Moon. As he stood for a moment looking at their beauty, he felt a hand on his shoulder and turned.

'You gave me the star freely,' said Alf. 'If you still wish to know to which child it will go, I will tell you.'

'I do indeed.'

'It shall go to any one that you appoint.'

The smith was taken aback and did not answer at once. 'Well,' he said hesitating, 'I wonder what you may think of my choice. I believe you have little reason to love the name of Nokes, but, well, his little great-grandson, Nokes of Townsend's Tim, is coming to the Feast. Nokes of Townsend is quite different.'

'I have observed that,' said Alf. 'He had a wise mother.'

'Yes, my Nell's sister. But apart from the kinship I love little Tim. Though he's not an obvious choice.'

Alf smiled. 'Neither were you,' he said. 'But I agree. Indeed I had already chosen Tim.'

'Then why did you ask me to choose?'

'The Queen wished me to do so. If you had chosen differently I should have given way.'

The smith looked long at Alf. Then suddenly he bowed low. 'I understand at last, sir,' he said. 'You have done us too much honour.'

'I have been repaid,' said Alf. 'Go home now in peace!'

When the smith reached his own house on the western outskirts of the village he found his son by the door of the forge. He had just locked it, for the day's work was done, and now he stood looking up the white road by which his father used to return from his journeys. Hearing footsteps he turned in surprise to see him coming from the village, and he ran forward to meet him. He put his arms about him in loving welcome.

'I've been hoping for you since yesterday, Dad,' he said. Then looking into his father's face he said anxiously: 'How tired you look! You have walked far, maybe?'

'Very far indeed, my son. All the way from Daybreak to Evening.'

They went into the house together, and it was dark except for the fire flickering on the hearth. His son lit candles, and for a while they sat by the fire without speaking; for a great weariness and bereavement was on the smith. At last he looked round, as if coming to himself, and he said: 'Why are we alone?'

His son looked hard at him. 'Why? Mother's over at Minor, at Nan's. It's the little lad's second birthday. They hoped you would be there too.'

'Ah yes. I ought to have been. I should have been, Ned, but I was delayed; and I have had matters to think of that put all else out of mind for a time. But I did not forget Tomling.'

He put his hand in his breast and drew out a little wallet of soft leather. 'I have brought him something. A trinket old Nokes maybe would call it – but it comes out of Faery, Ned.' Out of the wallet he took a little thing of silver. It was like the smooth stem of a tiny lily from the top of which came three delicate flowers, bending down like shapely bells. And bells they were, for when he shook them gently each flower rang with a small clear note. At the sweet sound the candles flickered and then for a moment shone with a white light.

Ned's eyes were wide with wonder. 'May I look at it, Dad?' he said. He took it with careful fingers and peered into the flowers. 'The work is a marvel!' he said. 'And, Dad, there is a scent in the bells: a scent that reminds me of, reminds me, well, of something I've forgotten.'

'Yes, the scent comes for a little while after the bells have rung. But don't fear to handle it, Ned. It was made for a babe to play with. He can do it no harm, and he'll take none from it.'

The smith put the gift back in the wallet and stowed it away. 'I'll take it over to Wootton Minor myself tomorrow,' he said. 'Nan and her Tom, and Mother, will forgive me, maybe. As for Tomling, his time has not come yet for the counting of days . . . and of weeks, and of months, and of years.'

'That's right. You go, Dad. I'd be glad to go with you; but it will be some time before I can get over to Minor. I couldn't have gone today, even if I hadn't waited here for you. There's a lot of work in hand, and more coming in.'

'No, no, Smith's son! Make it a holiday! The name of grandfather hasn't weakened my arms yet a while. Let the work come! There'll be two pair of hands to tackle it now, all working days. I shall not be going on journeys again, Ned: not on long ones, if you understand me.'

'It's that way is it, Dad? I wondered what had become of the star. That's hard.' He took his father's hand. 'I'm grieved for you; but there's good in it too, for this house. Do you know, Master Smith, there is much you can teach me yet, if you have the time. And I do not mean only the working of iron.'

They had supper together, and long after they had finished they still sat at the table, while the smith told his son of his last journey in Faery, and of other things that came to his mind – but about the choice of the next holder of the star he said nothing.

At last his son looked at him, and 'Father,' he said, 'do you remember the day when you came back with the Flower? And I said that you looked like a giant by your shadow. The shadow was the truth. So it was the Queen herself that you danced with! Yet you have given up the star. I hope it may go to someone as worthy. The child should be grateful.'

'The child won't know,' said the smith. 'That's the way with such gifts. Well, there it is. I have handed it on and come back to hammer and tongs.'

It is a strange thing, but old Nokes, who had scoffed at his apprentice, had never been able to put out of his mind the disappearance of the star in the Cake, although that event had happened so many years ago. He had grown fat and lazy, and retired from his office when he was sixty (no great age in the village). He was now near the end of his eighties, and was of enormous bulk, for he still ate heavily and doted on sugar. Most of his days, when not at table, he spent in a big chair by the window of his cottage, or by the door if it was fine weather. He liked talking, since he still had many opinions to air; but lately his talk mostly turned to the one Great Cake that he had made (as he was now firmly convinced), for whenever he fell asleep it came into his dreams. Prentice sometimes stopped for a word or two. So the old cook still called him, and he expected himself to be called Master. That Prentice was careful to do; which was a point in his favour, though there were others that Nokes was more fond of.

One afternoon Nokes was nodding in his chair by the door after his dinner. He woke with a start to find Prentice standing by and looking down at him. 'Hullo!' he said. 'I'm glad to see you, for that cake's been on my mind again. I was thinking of it just now in fact. It was the best cake I ever made, and that's saying something. But perhaps you have forgotten it.'

'No, Master. I remember it very well. But what is troubling you? It was a good cake, and it was enjoyed and praised.'

'Of course. I made it. But that doesn't trouble me. It's the little trinket, the star. I cannot make up my mind what became of it. Of course it wouldn't melt. I only said that to stop the children from being frightened. I have wondered if one of them did not swallow it. But is that likely! You might swallow one of those little coins and not notice it, but not that star. It was small but it had sharp points.'

'Yes, Master. But do you really know what the star was made of? Don't trouble your mind about it. Someone swallowed it, I assure you.'

'Then who? Well, I've a long memory, and that day sticks in it somehow. I can recall all the children's names. Let me think. It must have been Miller's Molly! She was greedy and bolted her food. She's as fat as a sack now.'

'Yes, there are some folk who get like that, Master. But Molly did not bolt her cake. She found two trinkets in her slice.'

'Oh, did she? Well, it was Cooper's Harry then. A barrel of a boy with a big mouth like a frog's.'

'I should have said, Master, that he was a nice boy with a large friendly grin. Anyway he was so careful that he took his slice to pieces before he ate it. He found nothing but cake.'

'Then it must have been that little pale girl, Draper's Lily. She used to swallow pins as a baby and came to no harm.'

'Not Lily, Master. She only ate the paste and the sugar, and gave the inside to the boy that sat next to her.'

'Then I give up. Who was it? You seem to have been watching very closely. If you're not making it all up.'

'It was the Smith's son, Master; and I think it was good for him.'

'Go on!' laughed old Nokes. 'I ought to have known you were having a game with me. Don't be ridiculous! Smith was a quiet slow boy then. He makes more noise now: a bit of a songster, I hear; but he's cautious. No risks for him. Chews twice before he swallows, and always did, if you take my meaning.'

'I do, Master. Well, if you don't believe it was Smith, can't help you. Perhaps it doesn't matter much now. Will ease your mind if I tell you that the star is back in the bo now? Here it is!'

Prentice was wearing a dark green cloak, which Nokes no noticed for the first time. From its folds he produced th black box and opened it under the old cook's nose. 'Ther is the star, Master, down in the corner.'

Old Nokes began coughing and sneezing, but at last h looked into the box. 'So it is!' he said. 'At least it looks lik it.'

'It is the same one, Master. I put it there myself few days ago. It will go back in the Great Cake thi winter.'

'A-ha!' said Nokes, leering at Prentice; and then h laughed till he shook like a jelly. 'I see, I see! Twenty-fou children and twenty-four lucky bits, and the star was on extra. So you nipped it out before the baking and kept it fc another time. You were always a tricky fellow: nimble on might say. And thrifty: wouldn't waste a bee's knee c butter. Ha, ha, ha! So that was the way of it. I might hav guessed. Well, that's cleared up. Now I can have a nap i peace.' He settled down in his chair. 'Mind that prentice man of yours plays you no tricks! The artful don't know a the arts, they say.' He closed his eyes.

'Goodbye, Master!' said Prentice, shutting the box wit such a snap that the cook opened his eyes again. 'Nokes he said, 'your knowledge is so great that I have only twic ventured to tell you anything. I told you that the star cam from Faery; and I have told you that it went to the smitl You laughed at me. Now at parting I will tell you one thin more. Don't laugh again! You are a vain old fraud, fat, idl and sly. I did most of your work. Without thanks yo learned all that you could from me – except respect for Faery, and a little courtesy. You have not even enough to bid me good day.'

'If it comes to courtesy,' said Nokes, 'I see none in calling your elders and betters by ill names. Take your Fairy and your nonsense somewhere else! Good day to you, if that's what you're waiting for. Now go along with you!' He flapped his hand mockingly. 'If you've got one of your fairy friends hidden in the Kitchen, send him to me and I'll have a look at him. If he waves his little wand and makes me thin again, I'll think better of him,' he laughed.

'Would you spare a few moments for the King of Faery?' the other answered. To Nokes's dismay he grew taller as he spoke. He threw back his cloak. He was dressed like a Master Cook at a Feast, but his white garments shimmered and glinted, and on his forehead was a great jewel like a radiant star. His face was young but stern.

'Old man,' he said, 'you are at least not my elder. As to my better: you have often sneered at me behind my back. Do you challenge me now openly?' He stepped forward, and Nokes shrank from him, trembling. He tried to shout for help but found that he could hardly whisper.

'No, sir!' he croaked. 'Don't do me a harm! I'm only a poor old man.'

The King's face softened. 'Alas, yes! You speak the truth. Do not be afraid! Be at ease! But will you not expect the King of Faery to do something for you before he leaves you? I grant you your wish. Farewell! Now go to sleep!'

He wrapped his cloak about him again and went away towards the Hall; but before he was out of sight the old cook's goggling eyes had shut and he was snoring.

When the old cook woke again the sun was going down. He

rubbed his eyes and shivered a little, for the autumn air was chilly. 'Ugh! What a dream!' he said. 'It must have been that pork at dinner.'

From that day he became so afraid of having more bad dreams of that sort that he hardly dared eat anything for fear that it might upset him, and his meals became very short and plain. He soon became lean, and his clothes and his skin hung on him in folds and creases. The children called him old Rag-and-Bones. Then for a time he found that he could get about the village again and walk with no more help than a stick; and he lived many years longer than he would otherwise have done. Indeed it is said that he just made his century: the only memorable thing he ever achieved. But till his last year he could be heard saying to any that would listen to his tale: 'Alarming, you might call it; but a silly dream, when you come to think of it. King o' Fairy! Why, he hadn't no wand. And if you stop eating you grow thinner. That's natural. Stands to reason. There ain't no magic in it.'

The time for the Twenty-four Feast came round. Smith was there to sing songs and his wife to help with the children. Smith looked at them as they sang and danced, and he thought that they were more beautiful and lively than they had been in his boyhood – for a moment it crossed his mind to wonder what Alf might have been doing in his spare time. Any one of them seemed fit to find the star. But his eyes were mostly on Tim: a rather plump little boy, clumsy in the dances, but with a sweet voice in the singing. At table he sat silent, watching the sharpening of the knife and the cutting of the Cake. Suddenly, he piped up: 'Dear Mr Cook, only cut me a small slice please. I've eaten so much already, I feel rather full.'

'All right, Tim,' said Alf. 'I'll cut you a special slice. I think you'll find it go down easily.'

Smith watched as Tim ate his cake slowly, but with evident pleasure; though when he found no trinket or coin in it he looked disappointed. But soon a light began to shine in his eyes, and he laughed and became merry, and sang softly to himself. Then he got up and began to dance all alone with an odd grace that he had never shown before. The children all laughed and clapped.

'All is well then,' thought Smith. 'So you are my heir. I wonder what strange places the star will lead you to? Poor old Nokes. Still I suppose he will never know what a shocking thing has happened in his family.'

He never did. But one thing happened at that Feast that pleased him mightily. Before it was over the Master Cook took leave of the children and of all the others that were present.

'I will say goodbye now,' he said. 'In a day or two I shall be going away. Master Harper is quite ready to take over. He is a very good cook, and as you know he comes from your own village. I shall go back home. I do not think you will miss me.'

The children said goodbye cheerfully, and thanked the Cook prettily for his beautiful Cake. Only little Tim took his hand and said quietly, 'I'm sorry.'

In the village there were in fact several families that did miss Alf for some time. A few of his friends, especially Smith and Harper, grieved at his going, and they kept the Hall gilded and painted in memory of Alf. Most people, however, were content. They had had him for a very long time and were not sorry to have a change. But old Nokes thumped his stick on the floor and said roundly: 'He's gone at last! And I'm glad for one. I never liked him. He was artful. Too nimble, you might say.'

The Homecoming of Beorhtnoth Beorhthelm's Son

The Homecoming of Beorhtnoth Beorhthelm's Son

I BEORHTNOTH'S DEATH

In August of the year 991, in the reign of Æthelred II, a battle was fought near Maldon in Essex. On the one side was the defence-force of Essex, on the other a viking host that had ravaged Ipswich. The English were commanded by Beorhtnoth son of Beorhthelm, the duke of Essex, a man renowned in his day: powerful, fearless, proud. He was now old and hoar, but vigorous and valiant, and his white head towered high above other men, for he was exceedingly tall.[1] The 'Danes' – they were on this occasion probably for the most part Norwegians – were, according to one version of the Anglo-Saxon Chronicle, led by Anlaf, famous in Norse saga and history as Olaf Tryggvason, later to become King of Norway.[2] The Northmen had sailed up the estuary of the Pante, now called the Blackwater, and encamped on Northey Island. The Northmen and the English were thus separated by an arm of the river; filled by the incoming tide, it could

[1] According to one estimate 6 foot 9 inches tall. This estimate was based on the length and size of his bones when examined, in his tomb at Ely, in A.D. 1769.

[2] That Olaf Tryggvason was actually present at Maldon is now thought to be doubtful. But his name was known to Englishmen. He had been in Britain before, and was certainly here again in 994.

only be crossed by a 'bridge' or causeway, difficult to force in the face of a determined defence.[1] The defence was resolute. But the vikings knew, or so it would seem, what manner of a man they had to deal with: they asked for leave to cross the ford, so that a fair fight could be joined. Beorhtnoth accepted the challenge and allowed them to cross. This act of pride and misplaced chivalry proved fatal. Beorhtnoth was slain and the English routed; but the duke's 'household', his *heorðwerod*, containing the picked knights and officers of his bodyguard, some of them members of his own family, fought on, until they all fell dead beside their lord.

A fragment – a large fragment, 325 lines long – of a contemporary poem has been preserved: it has no end and no beginning, and no title, but is now generally known as *The Battle of Maldon*. It tells of the demand of the vikings for tribute in return for peace; of Beorhtnoth's proud refusal, and challenge, and the defence of the 'bridge'; the cunning request of the vikings, and the crossing of the causeway; the last fight of Beorhtnoth, the falling of his golden-hilted sword from his maimed hand, and the hewing of his body by the heathen men. The end of the fragment, almost half of it, tells of the last stand of the bodyguard. The names, deeds, and speeches of many of the Englishmen are recorded.

The duke Beorhtnoth was a defender of the monks, and a patron of the church, especially of the abbey of Ely. After the battle the Abbot of Ely obtained his body and buried it in the abbey. His head had been hacked off and was not recovered: it was replaced in the tomb by a ball of wax.

According to the late, and largely unhistorical, account in

[1] According to the views of E. D. Laborde, now generally accepted. The causeway or 'hard' between Northey and the mainland is still there.

the twelfth-century *Liber Eliensis* the Abbot of Ely went himself with some of his monks to the battlefield. But in the following poem it is supposed that the abbot and his monks came only as far as Maldon, and that they there remained, sending two men, servants of the duke, to the battlefield some distance away, late in the day after the battle. They took a waggon, and were to bring back Beorhtnoth's body. They left the waggon near the end of the causeway and began to search among the slain: very many had fallen on both sides. Torhthelm (colloquially Totta) is a youth, son of a minstrel; his head is full of old lays concerning the heroes of northern antiquity, such as Finn, king of Frisia; Fróda of the Hatho-bards; Béowulf; and Hengest and Horsa, traditional leaders of the English Vikings in the days of Vortigern (called by the English Wyrtgeorn). Tídwald (in short Tída) was an old *ceorl*, a farmer who had seen much fighting in the English defence-levies. Neither of these men were actually in the battle. After leaving the waggon they became separated in the gathering dusk. Night falls, dark and clouded. Torh-thelm is found alone in a part of the field where the dead lie thick.

From the old poem are derived the proud words of Offa at a council before the battle, and the name of the gallant young Aelfwine (scion of an ancient noble house in Mercia) whose courage was commended by Offa. There also are found the names of the two Wulfmaers: Wulfmaer, son of Beorhtnoth's sister; and Wulfmaer the young, son of Wulf-stan, who together with Aelfnoth fell grievously hewn beside Beorhtnoth. Near the end of the surviving fragment an old retainer, Beorhtwold, as he prepares to die in the last desperate stand, utters the famous words, a summing up of the heroic code, that are here spoken in a dream by Torh-thelm:

> *Hige sceal þe heardra, heorte þe cenre,*
> *mod sceal þe mare þe ure maegen lytlað.*

'Will shall be the sterner, heart the bolder, spirit the greater as our strength lessens.'

It is here implied, as is indeed probable, that these words were not 'original,' but an ancient and honoured expression of heroic will; Beorhtwold is all the more, not the less, likely for that reason actually to have used them in his last hour.

The third English voice in the dark, speaking after the *Dirige* is first heard, uses rhyme: presaging the fading end of the old heroic alliterative measure. The old poem is composed in a free form of the alliterative line, the last surviving fragment of ancient English heroic minstrelsy. In that measure, little if at all freer (though used for dialogue) than the verse of *The Battle of Maldon*, the present modern poem is written.

The rhyming lines are an echo of some verses, preserved in the *Historia Eliensis*, referring to King Canute:

> Merie sungen ðe muneches binnen Ely,
> ða Cnut ching reu ðerby.
> 'Roweð, cnites, noer the land
> and here we ther muneches saeng.'

II THE HOMECOMING OF BEORHTNOTH BEORHTHELM'S SON

The sound is heard of a man moving uncertainly and breathing noisily in the darkness. Suddenly a voice speaks, loudly and sharply.

TORHTHELM   Halt! What do you want? Hell take you! Speak!

TÍDWALD   Totta! I know you by your teeth rattling.

TORHTHELM   Why, Tída, you! The time seemed long
alone among the lost. They lie so queer.
I've watched and waited, till the wind sighing
was like words whispered by waking ghosts
that in my ears muttered.

TÍDWALD   And your eyes fancied
barrow-wights and bogies. It's a black
   darkness
since the moon foundered; but mark my
   words:
not far from here we'll find the master,
by all accounts.

*Tídwald lets out a faint beam from a dark-lantern. An
owl hoots. A dark shape flits through the beam of light.
Torhthelm starts back and overturns the lantern, which
Tída had set on the ground.*

                     What ails you now?

TORHTHELM   Lord save us! Listen!

TÍDWALD   My lad, you're crazed.
Your fancies and your fears makes foes of
   nothing.
Help me to heave 'em! It's heavy labour
to lug them alone: long ones and short ones,
the thick and the thin. Think less, and talk
   less
of ghosts. Forget your gleeman's stuff!
Their ghosts are underground, or else God
   has them;
and wolves don't walk as in Woden's days,
not here in Essex. If any there be,
they'll be two-leggèd. There, turn him over!

An owl hoots again.

It's only an owl.

TORHTHELM   An ill boding.
Owls are omens. But I'm not afraid,
not of fancied fears. A fool call me,
but more men than I find the mirk gruesome
among the dead unshrouded. It's like the
      dim shadow
of heathen hell, in the hopeless kingdom
where search is vain. We might seek for ever
and yet miss the master in this mirk, Tída.
      O lord beloved, where do you lie tonight,
your head so hoar upon a hard pillow,
and your limbs lying in long slumber?

Tídwald lets out again the light of the dark-lantern.

TÍDWALD   Look here, my lad, where they lie thickest!
Here! lend a hand! This head we know!
Wulfmær it is. I'll wager aught
not far did he fall from friend and master.

TORHTHELM   His sister-son! The songs tell us,
ever near shall be at need nephew to uncle.

TÍDWALD   Nay, he's not here – or he's hewn out of ken.
It was the other I meant, th' Eastsaxon lad,
Wulfstan's youngster. It's a wicked business
to gather them ungrown. A gallant boy, too,
and the makings of a man.

TORHTHELM   Have mercy on us!
He was younger than I, by a year or more.

TÍDWALD   Here's Ælfnoth, too, by his arm lying.

TORHTHELM   As he would have wished it. In work or play
they were fast fellows, and faithful to their
      lord,
as close to him as kin.

TÍDWALD   Curse this lamplight
and my eyes' dimness! My oath I'll take
they fell in his defence, and not far away
now master lies. Move them gently!

TORHTHELM   Brave lads! But it's bad when bearded men
put shield at back and shun battle,
running like roe-deer, while the red heathen
beat down their boys. May the blast of
                Heaven
light on the dastards that to death left them
to England's shame! And here's Ælfwine:
barely bearded, and his battle's over.

TÍDWALD   That's bad, Totta. He was a brave lordling,
and we need his like: a new weapon
of the old metal. As eager as fire,
and as staunch as steel. Stern-tongued at
                times,
and outspoken after Offa's sort.

TORHTHELM   Offa! he's silenced. Not all liked him;
many would have muzzled him, had master
                let them.
'There are cravens at council that crow
                proudly
with the hearts of hens': so I hear he said
at the lords' meeting. As lays remind us:
'What at the mead man vows, when morning
                comes
let him with deeds answer, or his drink vomit
and a sot be shown.' But the songs wither,
and the world worsens. I wish I'd been here,
not left with the luggage and the lazy thralls,
cooks and sutlers! By the Cross, Tída,
I loved him no less than any lord with him;

and a poor freeman may prove in the end
more tough when tested than titled earls
who count back their kin to kings ere Woden.

TÍDWALD You can talk, Totta! Your time'll come,
and it'll look less easy than lays make it.
Bitter taste has iron, and the bite of swords
is cruel and cold, when you come to it.
Then God guard you, if your glees falter!
When your shield is shivered, between shame
     and death
is hard choosing. Help me with this one!
There, heave him over – the hound's
     carcase,
hulking heathen!

TORHTHELM   Hide it, Tída!
Put the lantern out! He's looking at me.
I can't abide his eyes, bleak and evil
as Grendel's in the moon.

TÍDWALD   Ay, he's a grim fellow,
but he's dead and done-for. Danes don't
     trouble me
save with swords and axes. They can smile or
     glare,
once hell has them. Come, haul the next!

TORHTHELM Look! Here's a limb! A long yard, and thick
as three men's thighs.

TÍDWALD   I thought as much.
Now bow your head, and hold your babble
for a moment, Totta! It's the master at last.
     There is silence for a short while.
Well, here he is – or what Heaven's left us:
the longest legs in the land, I guess.

TORHTHELM (*His voice rises to a chant.*)
    His head was higher than the helm of kings
    with heathen crowns, his heart keener
    and his soul clearer than swords of heroes
    polished and proven; then plated gold
    his worth was greater. From the world has
        passed
    a prince peerless in peace and war,
    just in judgement, generous-handed
    as the golden lords of long ago.
    He has gone to God glory seeking,
    Beorhtnoth beloved.

TÍDWALD   Brave words my lad!
    The woven staves have yet worth in them
    for woeful hearts. But there's work to do,
    ere the funeral begins.

TORHTHELM   I've found it, Tída!
    Here's his sword lying! I could swear to it
    by the golden hilts.

TÍDWALD   I'm glad to hear it.
    How it was missed is a marvel. He is marred
        cruelly.
    Few tokens else shall we find on him;
    they've left us little of the Lord we knew.

TORHTHELM Ah, woe and worse! The wolvish heathens
    have hewn off his head, and the hulk left us
    mangled with axes. What a murder it is,
    this bloody fighting!

TÍDWALD   Aye, that's battle for you,
    and no worse today than wars you sing of,
    when Fróda fell, and Finn was slain.
    The world weapt then, as it weeps today:
    you can hear the tears through the harp's
        twanging.

Come, bend your back! We must bear away
the cold leavings. Catch hold of the legs!
Now lift – gently! Now lift again!
They shuffle along slowly.

TORHTHELM   Dear still shall be this dead body,
though men have marred it.
Torhthelm's voice rises again to a chant.

Now mourn for ever
Saxon and English, from the sea's margin
to the western forest! The wall is fallen,
women are weeping; the wood is blazing
and the fire flaming as a far beacon.
Build high the barrow his bones to keep!
For here shall be hid both helm and sword;
and to the ground be given golden corslet,
and rich raiment and rings gleaming,
wealth unbegrudged for the well-beloved;
of the friends of men first and noblest,
to his hearth-comrades help unfailing,
to his folk the fairest father of peoples.
Glory loved he; now glory earning
his grave shall be green, while ground or sea,
while word or woe in the world lasteth.

TÍDWALD   Good words enough, gleeman Totta!
You laboured long as you lay, I guess,
in the watches of the night, while the wise
slumbered.
But I'd rather have rest, and my rueful
thoughts.
These are Christian days, though the cross is
heavy;
Beorhtnoth we bear not Béowulf here:
no pyres for him, nor piling of mounds;

and the gold will be given to the good abbot.
Let the monks mourn him and mass be
   chanted!
With learned Latin they'll lead him home,
if we can bring him back. The body's
   weighty!

TORHTHELM   Dead men drag earthward. Now down a spell!
My back's broken, and the breath has left me.

TÍDWALD   If you spent less in speech, you would speed
   better.
But the cart's not far, so keep at it!
Now start again, and in step with me!
A steady pace does it.
    Torhthelm halts suddenly.
                       You stumbling dolt,
Look where you're going!

TORHTHELM   For the Lord's pity,
halt, Tída, here! Hark now, and look!

TÍDWALD   Look where, my lad?

TORHTHELM   To the left yonder.
There's a shade creeping, a shadow darker
than the western sky, there walking crouched!
Two now together! Troll-shapes, I guess,
or hell-walkers. They've a halting gait,
groping groundwards with grisly arms.

TÍDWALD   Nameless nightshades – naught else can I see,
till they walk nearer. You're witch-sighted
to tell fiends from men in this foul darkness.

TORHTHELM   Then listen, Tída! There are low voices,
moans and muttering, and mumbled laughter.
They are moving hither!

TÍDWALD   Yes, I mark it now,
I can hear something.

TORHTHELM   Hide the lantern!

TÍDWALD   Lay down the body and lie by it!
            Now stone-silent! There are steps coming.

They crouch on the ground. The sound of stealthy steps
grows louder and nearer. When they are close at hand
Tídwald suddenly shouts out:

            Hullo there, my lads! You're late comers,
            if it's fighting you look for; but I can find
              you some,
            if you need it tonight. You'll get nothing
              cheaper.

There is a noise of scuffling in the dark. Then there is a
shriek. Torhthelm's voice rings out shrill.

TORHTHELM   You snuffling swine, I'll slit you for it!
            Take your trove then! Ho! Tída there!
            I've slain this one. He'll slink no more.
            If swords he was seeking, he soon found one,
            by the biting end.

TÍDWALD   My bogey-slayer!
            Bold heart would you borrow with
              Beorhtnoth's sword?
            Nay, wipe it clean! And keep your wits!
            That blade was made for better uses.
            You wanted no weapon: a wallop on the nose,
            or a boot behind, and the battle's over
            with the likes of these. Their life's wretched,
            but why kill the creatures, or crow about it?
            There are dead enough around. Were he a
              Dane, mind you,
            I'd let you boast – and there's lots abroad
            not far away, the filthy thieves:
            I hate 'em, by my heart, heathen or sprinkled,
            the Devil's offspring.

TORHTHELM   The Danes, you say!
    Make haste! Let's go! I'd half forgotten.
    There may be more at hand our murder
      plotting.
    We'll have the pirate pack come pouring on
      us,
    if they hear us brawling.

TÍDWALD   My brave swordsman!
    These weren't Northmen! Why should
      Northmen come?
    They've had their fill of hewing and fighting,
    and picked their plunder: the place is bare.
    They're in Ipswich now with the ale running,
    or lying off London in their long vessels,
    while they drink to Thor and drown the
      sorrow
    of hell's children. These are hungry folk
    and masterless men, miserable skulkers.
    They're corpse-strippers: a cursèd game
    and shame to think of. What are you
      shuddering at?

TORHTHELM Come on now quick! Christ forgive me,
    and these evil days, when unregretted
    men lie mouldering, and the manner of
      wolves
    the folk follow in fear and hunger,
    their dead unpitying to drag and plunder!
    Look there yonder! There's a lean shadow,
    a third of the thieves. Let's thrash the villain!

TÍDWALD Nay, let him alone! Or we'll lose the way.
    As it is we've wandered, and I'm bewildered
      enough.
    He won't try attacking two men by himself.

Lift your end there! Lift up, I say.
Put your foot forward.

TORHTHELM   Can you find it, Tída?
I haven't a notion now in these nightshadows
where we left the waggon. I wish we were
   back!

They shuffle along without speaking for a while.

Walk wary, man! There's water by us;
you'll blunder over the brink. Here's the
   Blackwater!
Another step that way, and in the stream
   we'd be
like fools floundering – and the flood's
   running.

TÍDWALD   We've come to the causeway. The cart's near
   it,
so courage, my boy. If we can carry him on
few steps further, the first stage is passed.
   They move a few paces more.
By Edmund's head! though his own's
   missing,
our Lord's not light. Now lay him down!
Here's the waggon waiting. I wish we could
   drink
his funeral ale without further trouble
on the bank right here. The beer he gave
was good and plenty to gladden your heart,
both strong and brown. I'm in a stew of
   sweat.
Let's stay a moment.

TORHTHELM   (*After a pause*)   It's strange to me
how they came across this causeway here,
or forced a passage without fierce battle;

but there are few tokens to tell of fighting.
A hill of heathens one would hope to find,
but none lie near.

TÍDWALD   No more's the pity.
Alas, my friend, our lord was at fault,
or so in Maldon this morning men were
    saying.
Too proud, too princely! But his pride's
    cheated,
and his princedom has passed, so we'll praise
    his valour.
He let them cross the causeway, so keen was
    he
to give minstrels matter for mighty songs.
Needlessly noble. It should never have been:
bidding bows be still, and the bridge
    opening,
matching more with few in mad handstrokes!
Well, doom he dared, and died for it.

TORHTHELM   So the last is fallen of the line of earls,
from Saxon lords long-descended
who sailed the seas, as songs tell us,
from Angel in the East, with eager swords
upon war's anvil the Welsh smiting.
Realms here they won and royal kingdoms,
and in olden days this isle conquered.
And now from the North need comes again:
wild blows the wind of war to Britain!

TÍDWALD   And in the neck we catch it, and are nipped
    as chill
as poor men were then. Let the poets babble,
but perish all pirates! When the poor are
    robbed

and lose the land they loved and toiled on,
they must die and dung it. No dirge for them,
and their wives and children work in serfdom.

TORHTHELM   But Æthelred'll prove less easy prey
than Wyrtgeorn was; and I'll wager, too,
this Anlaf of Norway will never equal
Hengest or Horsa!

TÍDWALD   We'll hope not, lad!
Come, lend your hand to the lifting again,
then your task is done. There, turn him
   round!
Hold the shanks now, while I heave the
   shoulders.
Now, up your end! Up! That's finished.
There cover him with the cloth.

TORHTHELM   It should be clean linen
not a dirty blanket.

TÍDWALD   It must do for now.
The monks are waiting in Maldon for us,
and the abbot with them. We're hours behind.
Get up now and in! Your eyes can weep,
or your mouth can pray. I'll mind the horses.
Gee up, boys, then. (*He cracks a whip.*) Gee
   up and away!

TORHTHELM   God guide our road to a good ending!

*There is a pause, in which a rumbling and a creaking
of wheels is heard.*

How these wheels do whine! They'll hear
   the creak
for miles away over mire and stone.

A longer pause in which no word is spoken.

Where first do we make for? Have we far to
   go?

<table>
<tr><td></td><td>The night is passing, and I'm near finished . . .
Say, Tída, Tída! is your tongue stricken?</td></tr>
<tr><td>TÍDWALD</td><td>I'm tired of talk. My tongue's resting.
'Where first' you say? A fool's question!
To Maldon and the monks, and then miles onward
to Ely and the abbey. It'll end sometime;
but the roads are bad in these ruinous days.
No rest for you yet! Were you reckoning on bed?
The best you'll get is the bottom of the cart
with his body for bolster.</td></tr>
<tr><td>TORHTHELM</td><td style="text-align:right">You're a brute, Tída.</td></tr>
<tr><td>TÍDWALD</td><td>It's only plain language. If a poet sang you:
'I bowed my head on his breast beloved,
and weary of weeping woeful slept I;
thus joined we journeyed, gentle master
and faithful servant, over fen and boulder
to his last resting and love's ending',
you'd not call it cruel. I have cares of my own
in my heart, Totta, and my head's weary.
I am sorry for you, and for myself also.
Sleep, lad, then! Sleep! The slain won't trouble,
if your head be heavy, or the wheels grumble.</td></tr>
</table>

He speaks to the horses.

Gee up, my boys! And on you go!
There's food ahead and fair stables,
for the monks are kind. Put the miles behind!

*The creaking and rattling of the waggon, and the
sound of hoofs, continue for some time, during which
no words are spoken. After a while lights glimmer in*

*the distance. Torhthelm speaks from the waggon,
drowsily and half dreaming.*

TORHTHELM　There are candles in the dark and cold voices.
I hear mass chanted for master's soul
In Ely isle. Thus ages pass,
and men after men. Mourning voices
of women weeping. So the world passes;
day follows day, and the dust gathers,
his tomb crumbles, as time gnaws it,
and his kith and kindred out of ken dwindle.
So men flicker and in the mirk go out.
The world withers and the wind rises;
the candles are quenched. Cold falls the night.

*The lights disappear as he speaks. Torhthelm's voice
becomes louder, but it is still the voice of one speaking
in a dream.*

It's dark! It's dark, and doom coming!
Is no light left us? A light kindle,
and fan the flame! Lo! Fire now wakens,
hearth is burning, house is lighted,
men there gather. Out of the mists they come
through darkling doors whereat doom
　　waiteth.
Hark! I hear them in the hall chanting:
stern words they sing with strong voices.
(*He chants*) Heart shall be bolder, harder be
　　purpose,
more proud the spirit as our power lessens!
Mind shall not falter nor mood waver,
though doom shall come and dark conquer.

There is a great bump and jolt of the cart.

Hey! what a bump, Tída! My bones are
　　shaken,

and my dream shattered. It's dark and cold.

TÍDWALD   Aye, a bump on the bone is bad for dreams,
and it's cold waking. But your words were queer,
Torhthelm my lad, with your talk of wind
and doom conquering and a dark ending.
It sounded fey and fell-hearted,
and heathenish, too: I don't hold with that.
It's night right enough; but there's no
    firelight:
dark is over all, and dead is master.
When morning comes, it'll be much like
    others:
more labour and loss till the land's ruined;
ever work and war till the world passes.

The cart rumbles and bumps on.

Hey! rattle and bump over rut and boulder!
The roads are rough and rest is short
for English men in Æthelred's day.

*The rumbling of the cart dies away. There is complete
silence for a while. Slowly the sound of voices chanting
begins to be heard. Soon the words, though faint, can
be distinguished.*

Dirige, Domine, in conspectu tuo viam
    meam.
Introibo in domum tuam: adorabo ad
    templum
Sanctum tuum in timore tuo.

(*A Voice in the dark*):   Sadly they sing, the monks of Ely
    isle!
Row men, row! Let us listen here a
    while!

*The chanting becomes loud and clear. Monks bearing a
bier amid tapers pass across the scene.*

Dirige, Domine, in conspectu tuo viam
meam.

Introibo in domum tuam: adorabo ad
templum sanctum tuum in timore tuo.

Domine, deduc me in iustitia tua: propter
inimicos meos

dirige in conspectu tuo viam meam.

Gloria Patri et Filio et Spiritui Sancto: sicut
erat in

principio et nunc et semper et in saecula
saeculorum.

Dirige, Domine, in conspectu tuo viam
meam.

They pass, and the chanting fades into silence.

III OFERMOD

THIS piece, somewhat larger than the Old English fragment
that inspired it, was composed primarily as verse, to be
condemned or approved as such.[1] But to merit a place in
Essays and Studies it must, I suppose, contain at least by
implication criticism of the matter and manner of the Old
English poem (or of its critics).

From that point of view it may be said to be an extended
comment on lines 89, 90 of the original: *ða se eorl ongan for
his ofermode alyfan landes to fela laþere ðeode*, 'then the earl
in his overmastering pride actually yielded ground to the
enemy, as he should not have done.' *The Battle of Maldon* has

[1] It was indeed plainly intended as a recitation for two persons,
two shapes in 'dim shadow', with the help of a few gleams of light
and appropriate noises and a chant at the end. It has, of course,
never been performed.

usually been regarded rather as an extended comment on, or illustration of the words of the old retainer Beorhtwold, 312, 313, cited above, and used in the present piece. They are the best-known lines of the poem, possibly of all Old English verse. Yet except in the excellence of their expression, they seem to me of less interest than the earlier lines; at any rate the full force of the poem is missed unless the two passages are considered together.

The words of Beorhtwold have been held to be the finest expression of the northern heroic spirit, Norse or English; the clearest statement of the doctrine of uttermost endurance in the service of indomitable will. The poem as a whole has been called 'the only purely heroic poem extant in Old English'. Yet the doctrine appears in this clarity, and (approximate) purity, precisely because it is put in the mouth of a subordinate, a man for whom the object of his will was decided by another, who had no responsibility downwards, only loyalty upwards. Personal pride was therefore in him at its lowest, and love and loyalty at their highest.

For this 'northern heroic spirit' is never quite pure; it is of gold and an alloy. Unalloyed it would direct a man to endure even death unflinching, when necessary: that is when death may help the achievement of some object of will, or when life can only be purchased by denial of what one stands for. But since such conduct is held admirable, the alloy of personal good name was never wholly absent. Thus Leofsunu in *The Battle of Maldon* holds himself to his loyalty by the fear of reproach if he returns home alive. This motive may, of course, hardly go beyond 'conscience': self-judgement in the light of the opinion of his peers, to which the 'hero' himself wholly assents; he would act the same, if there were no witnesses.[1] Yet this element of pride, in the form of the desire

[1] Cf. *Sir Gawain and the Green Knight*, 2127–31.

for honour and glory, in life and after death, tends to grow, to become a chief motive, driving a man beyond the bleak heroic necessity to excess – to chivalry. 'Excess' certainly even if it be approved by contemporary opinion, when it not only goes beyond need and duty, but interferes with it.

Thus Beowulf (according to the motives ascribed to him by the student of heroic-chivalric character who wrote the poem about him) does more than he need, eschewing weapons in order to make his struggle with Grendel a 'sporting' fight: which will enhance his personal glory; though it will put him in unnecessary peril, and weaken his chances of ridding the Danes of an intolerable affliction. But Beowulf has no duty to the Danes, he is still a subordinate with no responsibilities downwards; and his glory is also the honour of his side, of the Geatas; above all, as he himself says, it will redound to the credit of the lord of his allegiance, Hygelac. Yet he does not rid himself of his chivalry, the excess persists, even when he is an old king upon whom all the hopes of a people rest. He will not deign to lead a force against the dragon, as wisdom might direct even a hero to do; for, as he explains in a long 'vaunt', his many victories have relieved him of fear. He will only use a sword on this occasion, since wrestling singlehanded with a dragon is too hopeless even for the chivalric spirit. But he dismisses his twelve companions. He is saved from defeat, and the essential object, destruction of the dragon, only achieved by the loyalty of a subordinate. Beowulf's chivalry would otherwise have ended in his own useless death, with the dragon still at large. As it is, a subordinate is placed in greater peril than he need have been, and though he does not pay the penalty of his master's *mod* with his own life, the people lose their king disastrously.

In *Beowulf* we have only a legend of 'excess' in a chief.

The case of Beorhtnoth is still more pointed even as a story; but it is also drawn from real life by a contemporary author. Here we have Hygelac behaving like young Beowulf: making a 'sporting fight' on level terms; but at other people's expense. In his situation he was not a subordinate, but the authority to be obeyed on the spot; and he was responsible for all the men under him, not to throw away their lives except with one object, the defence of the realm from an implacable foe. He says himself that it is his purpose to defend the realm of Æthelred, the people, and the land (52–3). It was heroic for him and his men to fight, to annihilation if necessary, in the attempt to destroy or hold off the invaders. It was wholly unfitting that he should treat a desperate battle with this sole real object as a sporting match, to the ruin of his purpose and duty.

Why did Beorhtnoth do this? Owing to a defect of character, no doubt; but a character, we may surmise, not only formed by nature, but moulded also by 'aristocratic tradition', enshrined in tales and verse of poets now lost save for echoes. Beorhtnoth was chivalrous rather than strictly heroic. Honour was in itself a motive, and he sought it at the risk of placing his *heorðwerod*, all the men most dear to him, in a truly heroic situation, which they could redeem only by death. Magnificent perhaps, but certainly wrong. Too foolish to be heroic. And the folly Beorhtnoth at any rate could not wholly redeem by death.

This was recognised by the poet of *The Battle of Maldon*, though the lines in which his opinion is expressed are little regarded, or played down. The translation of them given above is (I believe) accurate in representing the force and implication of his words, though most will be more familiar with Ker's: 'then the earl of his overboldness granted ground

too much to the hateful people.'[1] They are lines in fact of
severe criticism, though not incompatible with loyalty, and
even love. Songs of praise at Beorhtnoth's funeral may well
have been made of him, not unlike the lament of the twelve
princes for Beowulf; but they too may have ended on the
ominous note struck by the last word of the greater poem:
lofgeornost 'most desirous of glory'.

So far as the fragment of his work goes, the poet of
Maldon did not elaborate the point contained in lines 89–90;
though if the poem had any rounded ending and final
appraisement (as is likely, for it is certainly not a work of
hot haste), it was probably resumed. Yet if he felt moved to
criticise and express disapproval at all, then his study of the
behaviour of the *heorðwerod* lacks the sharpness and tragic
quality that he intended, if his criticism is not fully valued.
By it the loyalty of the retinue is greatly enhanced. Their
part was to endure and die, and not to question, though a
recording poet may fairly comment that someone had blun-
dered. In their situation heroism was superb. Their duty was
unimpaired by the error of their master, and (more poignantly) neither in the hearts of those near to the old man was
love lessened. It is the heroism of obedience and love not of

[1] *To fela* means in Old English idiom that no ground at all should
have been conceded. And *ofermod* does not mean 'overboldness',
not even if we give full value to the *ofer*, remembering how strongly
the taste and wisdom of the English (whatever their actions)
rejected 'excess'. *Wita scal gepyldig . . . ne næfre gielpes to georn,
ær he geare cunne.* But *mod*, though it may contain or imply courage, does not mean 'boldness' any more than Middle English *corage.*
It means 'spirit', or when unqualified 'high spirit', of which the
most usual manifestation is pride. But in *ofer-mod* it is qualified,
with disapproval: *ofermod* is in fact always a word of condemnation.
In verse the noun occurs only twice, once applied to Beorhtnoth,
and once to Lucifer.

pride or wilfulness that is the most heroic and the most moving; from Wiglaf under his kinsman's shield, to Beorht-wold at Maldon, down to Balaclava, even if it is enshrined in verse no better than *The Charge of the Light Brigade*.

Beorhtnoth was wrong, and he died for his folly. But it was a noble error, or the error of a noble. It was not for his *heorðwerod* to blame him; probably many would not have felt him blameworthy, being themselves noble and chival-rous. But poets, as such, are above chivalry, or even heroism; and if they give any depth to their treatment of such themes, then, even in spite of themselves, these 'moods' and the objects to which they are directed will be questioned.

We have two poets that study at length the heroic and chivalrous, with both art and thought, in the older ages: one near the beginning in *Beowulf*; one near the end in *Sir Gawain*. And probably a third, more near the middle, in *Maldon*, if we had all his work. It is not surprising that any consideration of the work of one of these leads to the others. *Sir Gawain*, the latest, is the most fully conscious, and is in plain intention a criticism or valuation of a whole code of sentiment and conduct, in which heroic courage is only a part, with different loyalties to serve. Yet it is a poem with many inner likenesses to *Beowulf*, deeper than the use of the old 'alliterative'[1] metre, which is none the less significant. Sir Gawain, as the exemplar of chivalry, is of course shown to be deeply concerned for his own honour, and though the things considered honourable may have shifted or been enlarged, loyalty to word and to allegiance, and unflinching courage remain. These are tested in adventures no nearer to ordinary life than Grendel or the dragon; but Gawain's conduct is made more worthy, and more worth considering,

[1] It is probably the first work to apply the word 'letters' to this metre, which has in fact never regarded them.

again because he is a subordinate. He is involved in peril and the certain prospect of death simply by loyalty, and the desire to secure the safety and dignity of his lord, King Arthur. And upon him depends in his quest the honour of his lord and of his *heorðwerod*, the Round Table. It is no accident that in this poem, as in *Maldon* and in *Beowulf*, we have criticism of the lord, of the owner of the allegiance. The words are striking, though less so than the small part they have played in criticism of the poem (as also in *Maldon*). Yet thus spoke the court of the great King Arthur, when Sir Gawain rode away:

> *Before God 'tis a shame*
> *that thou, lord, must be lost, who art in life so noble!*
> *To meet his match among men, Marry, 'tis not easy!*
> *To behave with more heed would have behoved one of sense,*
> *and that dear lord duly a duke to have made,*
> *illustrious leader of liegemen in this land as befits him;*
> *and that better would have been than to be butchered to death,*
> *beheaded by an elvish man for an arrogant vaunt.*
> *Who ever heard tell of a king such courses taking,*
> *as knights quibbling at court at their Christmas games!*

Beowulf is a rich poem; there are of course many other sides to the description of the manner of the hero's death; and the consideration (sketched above) of the changing values of chivalry in youth and in age and responsibility is only an ingredient. Yet it is plainly there; and though the author's main imagination was moving in wider ways, criticism of the lord and owner of the allegiance is touched on.

Thus the lord may indeed receive credit from the deeds of his knights, but he must not use their loyalty or imperil them simply for that purpose. It was not Hygelac that sent

Beowulf to Denmark through any boast or rash vow. His words to Beowulf on his return are no doubt an alteration of the older story (which peeps rather through in the egging of the *snotere ceorlas*, 202–4); but they are the more significant for that. We hear, 1992–7, that Hygelac had tried to restrain Beowulf from a rash adventure. Very properly. But at the end the situation is reversed. We learn, 3076–83, that Wiglaf and the Geatas regarded any attack on the dragon as rash, and had tried to restrain the king from the perilous enterprise, with words very like those used by Hygelac long before. But the king wished for glory, or for a glorious death, and courted disaster. There could be no more pungent criticism in a few words of 'chivalry' in one of responsibility than Wiglaf's exclamation: *oft sceall eorl monig anes willan wraec adreogan*, 'by one man's will many must woe endure'. These words the poet of Maldon might have inscribed at the head of his work.

Also in Unwin Paperbacks

THE COMPLETE GUIDE TO MIDDLE-EARTH
Robert Foster

Middle-earth, the world in which the events of *The Hobbit, The Lord of the Rings* and *The Silmarillion* are set, is as real and complex as our own. Events, geography and names were created with care and loving attention by Tolkien, who wanted every single detail of his books to fit into their total pattern. A belief in perfection, the fun of sub-creation and the desire to create something so totally convincing that the reader could believe in it (in a sense) as actual history, involved him in map-making, endless charts of dates and events and the development of his many invented languages.

The Complete Guide to Middle-earth is intended to be supplementary to the works of Tolkien and no more. It draws together in logical sequence facts and information about names, languages, places and events from Tolkien's books and will be an indispensable aid in every reader's discovery of Tolkien's world.

J. R. R. TOLKIEN: A BIOGRAPHY
Humphrey Carpenter

In the authorised biography of J. R. R. Tolkien, Humphrey Carpenter draws upon Tolkien's private papers, diaries and manuscripts as well as interviews with family and friends to build up a fascinating portrait. He traces Tolkien's childhood, adolescence and war service and recounts how he achieved high repute as a scholar and university teacher.

Then sitting at his desk in Oxford one day he wrote: 'In a hole in the ground there lived a hobbit' – and soon found himself the author of a best-selling children's book. This book follows the long and painful process of creation that produced *The Lord of the Rings* and charts the growth of *The Silmarillion* and offers a wealth of information about Tolkien's life and work.